From Toxic Faitl

By Cath

Andrew & Jay:
May God richly
bless you as you
read of his great
deliverance.
Cathy Haggard

ISBN 978-0-578-43682-1
Library of Congress Catalog Card Number: 2018915187

Unless otherwise noted, Scripture quotations are from the New International Version of the Holy Bible. Copyright 1973, 1978, 1984 by International Bible Society.

In most instances names and places have been changed in this book.

Photograph of author by Gwen Bagne

Dedication

This book is dedicated to Joy Kirkpatrick, M.F.T, who faithfully cared and counseled me out of toxic faith into a living hope. There are no rewards on earth adequate to express my gratitude, so I pray you'll receive a crown with many jewels in heaven.

Endorsements

From Toxic Hope to a Living Faith is a completely engrossing and compelling story that paints a beautiful picture of our redemptive Jesus in a broken world. The author skillfully reminds us that being in Jesus's presence is where real life, real relationships, and real transformational experiences happen. This book challenges us to be with Jesus more so that we can know how intimate and altogether real Christ is in our lives.

Victor L. Obregon, M.D., MDiv., Husband, Father,
Pastor and Missionary

From Toxic Faith to a Living Hope is engaging, genuine, and brings hope. Cathy's testimony of God's healing power of love and hope are inspirational. Her story of God's willingness to enter into her pain and restore and heal the wounds where hope had died renews my anticipation for those who have reason to lose hope that renewal is possible. Cathy shares tangible, doable ways to walk in freedom and to thrive instead of just survive the challenges that life throws our way. A recommended reading, for sure.

Leila Faber, L.M.H.C.

I have known Cathy for many years and have watched first-hand the intimate relationship she shares with our heavenly Father, through Jesus, by the Holy Spirit. When she started telling me about her past and how the Lord had delivered her, I could hardly believe it. Her restoration has been so full that there are hardly any scars of her former ruin. I am grateful that Cathy has taken the time to share her journey, openly and transparently, in hopes that others will find the same freedom that she has experienced. I recommend *From Toxic Faith to a Living Hope* to anyone who has been hurt, anyone who feels his situation is hopeless, anyone who thinks he is beyond redemption, and anyone who wants a glimpse into what it means to walk in the wholeness that Jesus has made available for us.

Chiqui Polo-Wood, MDiv., DMin., Pastor,
International Author and Speaker

From Toxic Faith to a Living Hope is a beautiful autobiographical journey from the pain of toxic faith to the freedom of hope in Christ. The author shares firsthand experiences of what it's like to go from a works-based faith to a faith completely focused on the cross. It reminds us that no matter what we've been through, if we lean in to God, He will never leave us nor forsake us.

Joy Kirkpatrick, M.F.T.

From Toxic Faith to a Living Hope is an inspirational story of healing and transformation from the effects of abuse and rejection combined with bad religion. Cathy is vulnerable with her personal story as she shares her journey from pain and isolation to a discovery of Jesus truly being the answer in her life of healing, joy and family. The reading will walk away with renewed hope and powerful takeaways on learning how Jesus can be the answer for your life.

Pastor Craig Kessel, Pastoral Care Director
Northwest Church, Federal Way, Washington

Acknowledgments

I want to first thank my husband, Stephen Haggard, whose unwavering belief in me kept me going when I was uncertain on whether I could write this book. You are a part of my redemptive story, the love of my life and my best friend. I look forward to continuing our journey of hope together in Christ.

I want to thank my daughters, Chandra and Syona, your love and acceptance of me is part of the manifestation of Christ's living hope in my life.

I want to thank Tina Piety and Dr. Chiqui Polo-Wood for the fantastic editing job of this material. Your keen eyes and great advice enhanced the story in this book. You will share in God's blessing and rewards for everyone touched by reading this book.

I want to thank Brigit Larson for her editing advice early on in my writing. Your challenging words helped me find my voice.

I want to thank Mike and Linda Zeitner without them this story would not have happened. You showed me true love and faithfulness when I was broken, wounded and ever so needy. Thank you for your part in my healing process, your friendship and for encouraging me to write this book.

I want to thank Dr. Marty Folsom, my doctorate project mentor. You pushed me to write well, when I wanted to give up. This enabled me to not give up when writing this book was hard.

I want to thank Dr. Wes Pinkham, who reminded me of my story when religion was wanting to slowly steal it away.

I want to thank Colleen Danielson who read my manuscript and gave me valuable reader feedback and supported and encouraged me through the entire process.

There have been many other countless friends and family members that have been there for me as I wrote this book. I want to mention a few here. If your name is not mentioned it is only due to my poor memory, not my ungrateful heart. Thank you, Victor and Lori Obregon, for your friendship even across the miles. Thank you, Leila Faber, for listening to me over our lunches and never giving up on me. Thank you, Cindy Summerfield and Gwen Bagne, for all the hours of conversation that were essential for me to move forward. Thank you, Pastor Steve and Mary Schell, for giving me a safe environment at Northwest Church to heal. Thank you, Pastor Tomm Gordon, for believing in me and providing a way for me to grow in my writing.

Finally, I want to thank God the Father, who gave His Son for me that I might have life and know Him as my Abba. I want to thank Jesus Christ, who lifted me out of the miry clay of toxic faith and placed my feet on the solid rock. You are my precious Savior, Redeemer and my life. I want to thank the Holy Spirit who lives within me and is ever leading me into living hope.

Table of Contents

Introduction

I stood in the kitchen looking out the window. It was a bright, sunny, summer day. A soft gentle, warm breeze caused the vibrant flowers surrounding my rock house to move back and forth as if they were waving at me. The golden wheat prairie fields behind it swayed with the wind as if dancing in the field. The birds where chirping a lovely melody. Outside it was a beautiful, carefree day. Inside it was dark and gloomy. I was filled with such hopelessness. My despairing heart was unmoved by the flowers waving at me, the fields dancing, and the birds singing songs of life. I didn't know how to change my course. Nothing about my life was what I had longed for and lived for. My childhood dream I had since I was eleven years old had dissipated. It was the dream that had kept me going through all the trauma, abandonment, heartache, and abuse. It was an unshakable dream, or so I thought. I was sad, lonely, fearful, dejected, unwanted, friendless, and far away from the one person whom I always leaned on and felt so close to, Jesus. I felt like I had failed Him, that He was disappointed in me. Shame soaked my soul like a damp, wet rag. And now, the little church I had been attending for the past five years was dying. In a few short months the doors would be closing for good. I had sacrificed everything for this church and its organization. It had squeezed the life out of me and left me with nothing. I had become so entrenched in its distorted teaching that I believed I wouldn't make it to heaven unless I was a part of this organization. My soul and spirit where completely bound up. I had no joy, no peace. Because of this, I felt ashamed and embarrassed about being a Christian. Christians were supposed to have the answers, right? Yet, I had nothing to offer others. I had no answers.

I walked into the living room slumped down on the floor like a rag doll, leaning my arms and head upon the couch, I began to sob. Tears flowed down my cheek like a rushing river after a torrential rain. All I ever wanted in life was to walk with God, go to Bible School, and show the world who He was. Through my tears I cried out hopelessly to Him, "God I know you are the answer, I just don't know how." The tears flowed as if a dam had burst deep within my soul. I felt dejected and low. I knew that Jesus was deeply disappointed in me. I lifted my head, looked up and cried out to Him again, but this time with a new resolve. "God, I know you are the answer I just don't know how, but I want you to know that I will never let go of You no matter what, because I know You are the answer. I just don't know how." I laid my head down and sobbed uncontrollably. I did not know that the days ahead were going to get darker and this vow was going to be my sustaining grace.

Seven years after that dark day of my soul in the rock house. I sat in the sparsely decorated waiting room hoping I had made the right decision. The cold, stormy night echoed the turbulence inside my soul. Fear and anxiety raged within me. It was the first independent decision I had made in a very long time. I didn't know this person I was waiting for. Was she going to hurt me or help me? She finally opened the door and warmly welcomed me into her office. I wanted to run but knew that I had to stay.

I felt so small, like a tiny little girl sitting on an overstuffed couch. She grabbed her pen and paper, leaned forward and asked me with a cheerful voice, "How can I help you?"

I looked down at the floor, wrung my hands, the words were hard to formulate, but finally I slowly said, "I need help and don't tell me to just trust Jesus." I slowly looked up to see her response. Her eyes were full of compassion and grace, yet she seemed surprised by my answer. I had been a Christian since I was five years old, but here I sat, twenty-five years later, needing help; I needed someone to help me find the Jesus I met at five years old and had lost in the midst of life and the church. I still believed He was the answer, but in my Christian walk so far, I hadn't discovered how. Deep inside I was hoping she would help me discover how but was afraid I would get the same old teachings that had brought me to this place.

That night was the beginning of a season of transformational healing from many kinds of abuses and abandonments that had led me into what I discovered to be toxic faith. Toxins are poisons that bring forth death. My childhood abuses created a vulnerability in my faith causing me to be susceptible to spiritual toxins that poisoned my faith and robbed me of joy and hope. God used my counselor and others to help me discover how Jesus truly is the answer and led me into a living hope. Over time my soul and spirit became healed, whole, and solid. In Part I of this book, I tell my story of how I became overwhelmed and controlled by toxic faith. Then in Part II, I'll share different encounters I had with Truth and the Giver of truth that transformed and healed my heart and soul, revealing to me how Jesus is the answer and imparted to me living hope.

It wasn't through brilliant teaching, fabulous worship, or a great church service that I learned how Jesus is the answer. The pathway wasn't linear. I can't give you a three-step, or five-step process of healing because true healing comes out of relationship with the living God; therefore, the healing chapters in Part II are not meant to be interpreted as sequential steps of healing, although some truths opened me up to other truths. It is my prayer that as you read these chapters, you too will encounter Jesus, receive healing, learn how He is the answer amid this broken world ridden with toxic faith, and experience living hope.

Part I

≈1≈

Faith Born

It was a pleasant sunny afternoon; my father sat in his comfortable chair, relaxing. I approached him and waited for him to welcome me onto his lap. He was happy to see me and gave me a big hug as he lifted me up. I was only five years old, but I loved to hear Daddy tell stories; he was a remarkable story teller. I would plead with him to tell me about Moses and then to tell me about Noah. He would faithfully tell me the stories repeatedly, no matter how many times I asked him. On this particular day, after he told me the stories, I began to cry. They were gut wrenching tears. Dad held me close and gently asked, "What's wrong?" Between my sobs and tears I told him, "I want to be just like Jesus." A seed of love and unshakeable faith was planted deep within my heart that day. My faith was simple and real. My heart became solidly fixed on Jesus that afternoon. From that day forward, I desired nothing more than to be like Jesus and serve Him.

When I was eight, I was baptized in water in Center Creek. I remember it being such a glorious day. The sun was shining, hiding the fact that the water, like all creeks in southwest Missouri, was icy cold, but I didn't care. I went down under the water and came up feeling so much joy; I thought my heart would burst. This was a step of becoming more like Jesus. As soon as the short river-side service was over, I hopped in the back of the pickup and wrapped a towel around my shivering body. My heart was so full. Tears began to flow down my cheeks and my young heart broke out in silent worship and praise to God. I loved Him so much and wanted to be near Him. Nothing else mattered in my eight-year-old heart.

My spiritual life and journey seemed to be on track at such an early age; however, there were many things brewing in my life that would ultimately impact my spiritual journey in ways that at this age, I could never imagine.

≈2≈

Faulty Foundation

I heard the kitchen door slam behind me as I rushed out of the rock house and down the patio stairs. I grabbed my bicycle, hopped on and rode as fast as my little feet could pedal. With tears streaming down my checks, my heart was pounding, and my thoughts were racing as I rode my bike as fast and furiously as I could towards my best friend's house. Mom and Dad had just announced that we were moving, AGAIN! This would be our tenth move since I was born, nine years earlier. I thought the days of moving were over. In the first seven years of my life, we moved nine times. My dad had suffered several serious illnesses. He was in and out of hospitals multiple times and had a challenging time even holding down a job. However, at age seven, we had finally settled into a community. We lived in a rock house on the edge of town. I had a friend for the first time in my life. I was learning to play the piano. I was taking gymnastics lessons. I was involved and strongly connected. I loved the little church we were attending. My faith in Jesus was strong and growing. I had allowed my little roots to plant deeply into this community, this home. And now we were moving. My world was rocked.

As I raced to my friend's house, I anxiously looked at my familiar surroundings realizing that I would never see these trees again, these houses, this road, the local gas station, my friend. Panic hit me; my heart was racing faster and faster. Everything inside me began to scream, "BUT I NEED THESE THINGS!" I kept repeating it over and over again pedaling my bicycle faster and faster, my heart

7

pounding just as fast. Then, as quickly as I ran out the door, I slammed on my bicycle breaks and came to a screeching halt. I stood there in silence, panting, trying to catch my breath. My thoughts eventually landed on a startling realization. My nine-year-old mind concluded, "Wait a minute, I mustn't really need any of these things. I mustn't really need my friend, my home, my community because if I did, then my parents wouldn't do this to me. They wouldn't move me from this place and from my friend if I truly needed them." My heart sunk deep into my soul with this new-found revelation. Darkness began to overshadow the light.

That dark day marked the end of any sense of stability and normality in my childhood. We resumed our lifestyle of constantly moving. My dad's inability to hold down a job and subsequent financial troubles plagued us all our lives. I never knew when I came home from school if that would be my last day because we'd be moving again the next day. I never knew if there would be food on the table, electricity, gas, or even water, due to the utilities being turned off. Sometimes we'd live days without a utility. Being without water was the hardest, (this was before you could buy bottled water). I remember coming home from shopping and the landlord had changed the locks on the doors to our home because the rent wasn't paid. He only allowed us in to move out. During a period where we couldn't pay for the garbage to be picked up, the garbage builds up so long in the garage that we had maggots everywhere. It was humiliating as we washed them out of the garage and down the sewer drains in the street, as the neighbors stood by watching. It was a life of continual disruption, loss, and chaos. I felt insecure, embarrassed, ashamed, afraid and angry. I didn't know what the next day would entail. By the time I graduated from high school, I had lived in twenty-three different houses, ten different cities and three different states. The meeting of one's basic needs is core to building a solid internal foundation in one's soul. My foundation was made up of crumbled debris. The only thing that had any sense of security was my relationship with God, which I clung onto for dear life.

That day, when I was nine years old, redefined me and my idea of needs. On that day, something inside of me died. My view of life, my surroundings and people all changed. I began to lose my ability to bond and care. In the years following that dreadful day, I would try to become involved with things like baseball, Girl Scouts, even church events, only to be pulled out of these, due to moving or some other embarrassing situation. Eventually, I stopped trying. I never experienced friendships again because it is impossible to develop any kind of friendship when you are only present for a short-time.

Even though we changed churches more frequently than we changed houses, my heart clung onto the Jesus I had met when I was five and my passion and longing to be like Him never wavered. At the age of eleven, I accepted the call into ministry. My course was set in my young heart and I never considered or desired a different path. I was going to go to Bible college and serve in full-time ministry. Not just any Bible college, I was going to go to L.I.F.E. Bible college in Los Angeles, CA. However, the instability, dysfunction, and abuses in my childhood took a toll on my soul that crippled me spiritually in ways I didn't realize. Jesus was who I clung onto to survive rather than to live and thrive.

This lifestyle also took a great toll on my parents' marriage. They began to fight constantly. I remember one evening when I was thirteen, my brother, sisters, and I curled up on one of our beds and listened to them fight till late in the night. We began to wonder how long it would be before they would divorce, and we talked about what we would do. We longed for them to divorce, hoping that would bring peace. This lifestyle and my parents' fighting affected each one of us kids differently. Bobby, my brother, who was the oldest, became angry and full of violence. Becky, my older sister, became angry and bitter. Lori, my little sister, too young to really understand any of what was going on, became angry and rebellious. I became angry and withdrawn. During this time, I would retreat into my room and get my hymnal and sing songs to God or read my Bible and pray. This was my sustaining force.

Although I clung to Jesus, I found myself shutting down more and more to the world around me because of the instability, abuse, and great losses. At age fourteen, the pain of constant chaos and loss caused me to take a vow to never like anything anymore in my life. I wouldn't hate anything either, because Christians aren't supposed to hate. I just became numb and neutral about life and my surroundings. I felt aloneness, rejection, dejection, shame, worthlessness, unwanted, and unloved. Fear and shame dominated my life. The only thing that gave me any sense of worth was my relationship with Jesus, my confidence of the call into ministry, and my plan to go to Bible college. This is what I clung to; this is where I found hope.

I was fifteen when my parents finally separated. Only we three girls were living at home at the time. My brother was in the Coast Guard. My father initiated this event. He privately asked each of girls who we wanted to live with when they separated. We all chose to live with Dad. Dad appeared to be the safer of the two and didn't treat us like slaves. This was a real blow to my mother, who felt like her life was being ripped apart by my father's decision. Even though all of us kids could see this day coming for years, it took her by surprise. My older sister, who had just turned eighteen, left the home immediately after the separation, to get out of the crossfires, leaving my little sister and I to go through the volatile months that lay ahead, leading to the divorce.

Shortly after the separation and decision on my father's part to get a divorce, my mother kidnapped my little sister. It was a terrifying time. We didn't know where she was or what was happening. Dad was desperate to find her and get her back. I just hid in the shadows, full of fear and anxiety, hoping no harm had come to her. Dad finally found her with mom. She was returned to my dad.

This incident motivated Dad to pursue temporary custody of Lori and me. We peeked through the windows into the courtroom, watching as mom and dad each took the stand, afraid to enter the room. I was so glad I could not hear anything that was being said. After the judge heard their side, she took Lori and I into her chambers.

The room was full of books, floor to ceiling. Lori and I sat on the couch. I felt so small. The judge was a kind, gentle lady. She started with me. "Who do you want to live with?" Without hesitation, I told her my dad. I loved and adored my dad. I feared and hated my mother. I sat and told her about my mother treating us like slaves and her uncontrollable behavior when she and dad fought. She then leaned over and asked Lori. Lori agreed with me.

We left the judge's chambers and ran into the bathroom. We didn't want to see our mom when she came out. Becky, my older sister instructed us to get in the stall, lock them and then stand on the toilet so if mother came in, she wouldn't see us in there. We did. It was quiet and eerie as we waited for the all clear sign. It finally came. We ran out to greet Dad, who gave us the good news that he was awarded temporary custody. We all went home believing that chapter was over.

Shortly after this, Dad met a woman at work. He fell head over heels in love with Nancy and she with him. However, in her mind, we were extra baggage that she didn't want around. Dad would spend all his spare time with her, leaving Lori and me alone day after day. This only intensified my sense of aloneness.

The courts required Lori to see our mom every other weekend, but in my case, they left it to my own discretion on whether I saw mother or not. I chose not to see her. I wanted nothing to do with her. The anger and hatred that had been brewing in my heart towards her for years had found a way out, and it consumed me. Her abusive treatment of us kids caused my heart to pull away from her in favor of my dad. I loved and admired my dad and believed that she was the one at fault.

One cold, rainy winter night, Dad and I went to pick up Lori at my mother's apartment. I could see my parents fighting under the glow of the porch light. Dad and Lori returned to the car. I had never seen my dad so angry. Through all the fighting growing up, Dad was always the calm controlled one and Mom was the hysterical one. But tonight, I saw a dark side of Dad I had never seen before. Lori jumped in the back seat while I rode in the front. Dad was seething with anger as he drove off. He began to yell at my little sister. She was eleven and looked so small in the back seat of our huge car. At one point he told her that he was so angry that if he wasn't driving, he would kill her. I froze when I heard those words; fear swept over my whole being. I couldn't help but think of my little sister all alone in the back seat which almost swallowed her up. I could only imagine how those words pierced her little eleven-year-old heart and shattered her world. It was only a few months earlier, when Mother tried to kill us by grabbing the wheel of the car from Dad, trying to force the car off an embankment. She would've rather seen us dead then to go through the separation and subsequent divorce. Dad became the "safe one" when he regained control of the car and rescued us. Now, the safe parent also expressed a desire to kill. I shrunk back with fear, withdrawing inside myself, hanging onto the Jesus I met at five years old. Dad turned the car around and took Lori back to Mom and left her there, never to see her again. Now, I was all alone. I only had Dad. I had lost all my siblings during the crossfire, was estranged from my mother, and Dad was consumed with a new love.

By this time, we had moved in with my dad's new girlfriend, but Nancy made it very clear that I wasn't wanted. They began to have fights regarding me. She begged him to get rid of me and threatened to leave him if he didn't. Each night when I got home, I would retreat into the formal living room. I would turn out all the lights wanting so desperately to be loved and accepted by Dad and Nancy but fearing that if I made too much noise or appearance I would be rejected. My goal was to just be kept. The darkness in the room matched the pain and darkness in my soul. The only glimpse of light was the kitchen light shining into the room. I laid on the couch listening to a worship song that expressed God's love and power in my situation.

I would listen to this song over and over again, tears flowing down my cheeks. I soaked in the words like a parched land soaks up fresh rain. Though ever so small, eventually my soul would feel hope and strength rise up again within me to live another day. It was in those moments of intimacy with God, that the world finally seemed right, but just for a moment.

The divorce was finalized on February 14, shortly after my sixteenth birthday. Dad and Nancy married fourteen days later. They hadn't fought over me for some weeks now, so I thought that my place with them was secure. All I ever wanted was my dad. I wanted to live with him and be loved by him. While they were on their honeymoon, I stayed with my older sister, Becky. What I didn't know was that Dad wanted to leave me there, but Becky refused. When Dad and Nancy returned, they picked me up and we moved to a new house, in a new town, to begin a new life as a new family. Although I missed my siblings, I was excited to start this new life, believing all the pain from the past would be gone and I'd find happiness, love, and acceptance. But my dream of a new life with Dad and his new wife, and my hope for love, acceptance, and happiness quickly came to an end.

It was our first night in our new place. Nancy couldn't cook, so I cooked us a spaghetti dinner. Everything seemed good. I felt happy and hopeful for the first time in a very long time. I thought the struggles between her and I were over and didn't expect what was to happen next. Dad excused himself from the table, leaving us alone. Nancy stretched out her hand and flashed her diamond/ruby cluster ring in front of me. "Isn't my ring beautiful?" she asked. I admired it and then responded, "Yes, it is very beautiful, but when I get married, I want a simple ring with a simple diamond." She abruptly pulled back her hand and stormed off. I had insulted her for the last time. I was stunned. I thought I was having a friendly conversation with her. I felt no malice towards her, but she was insulted by my comment. From that day forward, Dad and Nancy not only refused to talk to me, except out of necessity, but they also refused to be in the same room with me. If I came into a room, they would abruptly leave the room. If they wanted to come into a room that I was in, they would wait until I was gone. The home was icy cold and very dark. The aloneness from the shunning was deafening. The only warmth that I felt was in my room, which was filled with God's presence and love. It was God's sustaining presence that kept me going when I felt so alone, shunned, and rejected. I couldn't figure out what I had done wrong, so I could only conclude that I was what was wrong.

At the end of two weeks, Dad hesitantly entered my room and explained to me that I could no longer live with him. He didn't want me to live with my mother, which I didn't want to either, but I couldn't live with him. He explained to me how I was sixteen and many sixteen-year-olds where living on their own and he knew I could do the same. I sat there taking it all in, acting so brave, but inside I was terrified. I could barely function, how was I to live on my own? He had arranged for me to live with his sister, Aunt June, until I got on my feet. There was nothing I could do but say, "Yes, Daddy." I lay in bed that night and fear gripped my soul. I didn't know what was going to happen to me. I only knew to cling to God.

I had been at my aunt's house for three days. It was a deplorable situation. Cockroaches had overtaken the house. They were everywhere, even in the bed. I was afraid and didn't know the first thing to do to make it on my own. I would cry uncontrollably at times. Aunt June ignored me most of the time, but other times tried to comfort me the best she could. After three days, she finally took me to a payphone so that I could call my dad. I waited anxiously for him to pick up. The minute he said hello, I began to sob uncontrollably, "Daddy, I want to live with you. Please come and get me." I don't know how long I cried, nor what all was said, I only remember the words, "OK, I'll pick you up in the morning." My heart was elated! I skipped back to the car. My daddy was coming to get me. All was going to be well now. I slept that night in peace for the first time in a long time.

That next morning, I danced and skipped around the house so excited that Dad was coming to pick me up. Now I would live with him; he would love me and want me. That is all I ever desired. I was constantly peeking out the window any time a car turned onto our street, wondering if it was Dad. Finally, his car pulled up. I ran out with great excitement and anticipation ready to jump into his arms and feel safe but was confronted with the unexpected. He stood coldly next to the open car door and told me to jump in. There was no hug, no smile. Nancy sat in the front seat looking straight ahead with a stern face, not even giving me a glance. The car was full of boxes; I was bewildered. We went for a drive and Dad began to yell at me, but I was in such a state of shock I couldn't comprehend the words he was saying. I just know they pierced deep into my heart creating a crevice-like wound so deep that no light could shine into it. We returned shortly to my aunt's house. Dad unloaded the boxes that had my belongings in them. I leaned against them in shock and unbelief. Dad looked straight into my eyes and said with great intensity, "I never want to see you again. If I do, I'll let you know. You are never to call me or look me up. I never want to see you again!" I sat in silent disbelief. Unable to speak, yet, my heart responded on the inside, "OK Daddy, if that will make you happy. I just want to make you happy. It's OK Daddy, I have Jesus." He turned, hopped into his car and drove off. I watched his car get smaller and smaller as it drove down the road and fade into the horizon. I stood there wondering what I was going to do when my broken heart felt the gentle assurance of the One who had always been there for me, Jesus. I didn't know how, but I knew that I would be ok because He was with me.

I knew I couldn't stay at my aunt's house nor survive on my own. My dad's final decision to abandon me at Aunt June's doorstep forced me into a decision I didn't want to make. I had to find Mom and return to her. That brought shivers down my spine, but I didn't know any other way to survive. I hadn't seen her in six months and was uncertain of her whereabouts, but my grandmother lived close to my aunt, so the next day, I would walk to my grandmother's home and inquire where Mom lived. With my plan in place, I hunkered down for one last night at Aunt June's house. While we were watching television, we heard a knock on the door. To our surprise, it was my mother. She hadn't seen my aunt in several months, but tonight felt like she needed to stop by to say hello. She was living nearby with my grandmother. I was surprised and relieved to see her. She packed up my things, put them in her car, and we returned to grandmother's house. We never talked about what had happened to me. She never inquired, and I never felt safe to tell her. She brought me home like a conqueror brings home the spoils after a great battle. To her, I represented victory over my dad, which only intensified my painful experience. I wanted love, comfort, and safety; instead, I received gloating over the defeat and conquest of my dad. She had won the battle and had all her children on her side, at least so she thought. But I wasn't on her side; I was just trying to survive.

≈3≈

Turbulent Times

The kitchen chairs tumbled to the floor as the two of them jumped from the table flinging plates and glasses across the room. Their voices escalated to a violent intensity. My twenty-year-old brother grabbed my twelve-year-old sister and flung her across the room into the wall. This wasn't their first violent fight. Bobby had received an honorable hardship discharge from the Coast Guard to return home to help mother, yet his violent temper brought more harm than help. All his anger towards our childhood and our parents was now being taken out on our little sister. He often beat her, flung her across the room and threw her against the wall with such force her foot or arm would go through the wall. Once I watched as he threw her on the bed and backhanded her so hard that it cracked her ribs. In the past, I was paralyzed with fear and helplessness, but this fight was different. Lori screamed as she raced through the living room back to her bedroom. I knew this time he would kill her. I had to do something, there was no way out from the back of the house. I jumped off the couch and stood in the entrance to the hallway to her room. I could hear her screaming in the background. She was so full of fear. My brother came charging out of the kitchen only to find me in his pathway. He put his hands around my throat and glared into my eyes. His rage was so intense that his nostrils flared, and his breathing caused his body to heave. I knew I was only a moment away from great harm, but I also knew that I had to save my sister's life. I looked straight into his eyes, "Bobby, go outside." Under my breath I said,

"In the name of Jesus I take authority over you." Then I would pause. I repeated this again and again while his hands held my throat and his enraged eyes glared at me. This moment felt like an eternity, but eventually my brother silently turned around and went outside. My knees gave way beneath me as I crumbled to the floor, my heart full of gratitude that God had rescued me and my little sister.

Mom, full of grief and pain, was incapacitated when it came to deal with the violence in the home. She was either not around or too afraid herself. Her bitterness and desire for revenge towards my dad consumed her. She found herself left to find her own way as a single mom with no work history or skills, while Dad was off living a new life, with a new wife. Mom was difficult to live with before the divorce, but all this new-found pain, anger, hate, and grief made it even more difficult. The one person that I should have been able to find comfort in, became the one person I had to protect myself from the most.

Mom communicated in what I call a sideways manner. She was never direct but maneuvered and manipulated things to try to get what she wanted. She knew that I had a tender heart for God, so she would use God and His Word to manipulate me. One of these times was after my first date with Jim. He gave me a gentle kiss good-night and turned and walked away. I felt like I was floating a few inches off the floor as I walked into the house. We had been admiring each other for some time now and it finally happened. I was looking forward to curling up in bed, rehearsing the evening and dozing off with a smile on my face. I knew I would see him again. My afterglow was immediately shattered as I heard my mother yell my name and order me into her room. She spent most of her time at home either in front of the television or in bed. As I started walking towards her, she told me to grab my Bible and bring it with me. I sat on the edge of her bed uncertain of what was to come. She asked me to read the Ten Commandments. I found where they were and read them.

"Now, which one did you break tonight?"

I was shocked. I felt a sweat break out and my mind began to race, "What did she mean? What did she think I had done?" I finally responded, "None of them."

"Read them again." So, I did. "Now, which one did you break tonight?"

My feeling of delight and pleasure from my date was replaced by anxiety and fear. I knew I had done nothing wrong on my date, but her pounding persistence squeezed the innocence out of it. I repeated with a sterner voice, "None of them."

"Read them again." This was repeated several times until finally she asked, "Isn't there one that states, thou shalt not lie?"

Now I was getting frustrated. Surely, she wanted me to confess something, but I didn't know what it was. After a few more times of reading the Ten Commandments and telling her I hadn't done anything wrong, what she was accusing me of finally came out. She thought I had been in contact with my dad and knew where he was. This whole thing didn't have anything to do with my date and yet, I felt tortured over it. I explained to her that I didn't know where my dad was, then abruptly got up and ran to my room, and cried myself to sleep.

Tears were my constant companion during this season of living with my mom, Bobby, and Lori. I cried myself to sleep almost every night. My soul and spirit were being battered repeatedly, making it more difficult to want to live, and my hope began to dwindle. With each day that passed, I found myself withdrawing deeper and deeper within myself until I was a mere shell of a person. I clung to God to survive. The only dream I had left in me was the dream of going to Bible school and doing something significant for God. The only safe place I found was at church, but that began to change on one unforgettable afternoon.

I excitedly entered the building and hurried down the hall. I was meeting with Pastor Lenny today to discuss the youth group. Unlike my home life, my life at the church was happy and fulfilling. I was beginning to experience what my heart had dreamed of and believed for amid all the pain. It was the first time since that dark day, many years ago, that I felt like I belonged and had purpose. Even though I was just a teen myself, the pastor allowed me to be the youth group leader. When I started, three months earlier, there were only six teenagers and now there were thirty-five. Things were happening, and it was an exciting time. I made my way through the sanctuary and into Pastor Lenny's study. As I entered the room, I was surprised to find a nice-looking young man named Max sitting in one of the chairs. Pastor Lenny directed me to sit in the chair next to him and made the introductions. I quickly acknowledged him but was so excited to report all the good things that were happening that I barely gave him any recognition. However, before I could even open my mouth, Pastor Lenny began to explain how I could no longer be the leader of the youth group. I felt perplexed and didn't understand. Everything was going so well. My heart began to sink and all the excitement I felt drained out of me. Max had just returned after a one-year absence, and he wanted to be over the youth group. Pastor Lenny explained to me that I was only allowed to be over the youth group because there was no man or boy to do it. But now that Max had returned and wanted to be over the youth group, I had to step down because I was a woman. I was dumbfounded. It didn't matter how well I was doing or how the youth group was growing. All that mattered, in this decision, was that I was a woman and he was a man. I had no choice but to resign. However, under Max's leadership, the youth group quickly dwindled down to around eight to ten teenagers, and it never grew again. My heart was very sad. This was the first time I experienced rejection within the church, but it wasn't to be my last.

Pastor Lenny's decision pierced into my soul and spirit and plagued me for years. It affirmed the devaluation, rejection, and abandonment from my childhood. Now my childhood pain had entered the one place I tried so hard to keep it out of – my dreams of Bible school, ministry, and my relationship with God.

Things at home continued to worsen and I became more and more mechanical and withdrawn. By the time I graduated from high school, I didn't have the life skills I needed to be successful and follow my dreams. The only skills I had learned were how to survive in a chaotic world by withdrawing from the world. Life and the world around me became something I feared. So, when Pastor Lenny took me and another girl to a Bible college campus in the east, I was flooded with immobilizing fear. I didn't know how to function or operate in the normal world. I didn't know how to make friends or interact with others. I didn't know the first thing of how to live and thrive. My fear became greater than my dream and I convinced the pastor to take me back home, leaving my dream that I had clung to for survival, behind.

It was a long ride home. The silence in the car was deafening. I could feel the intense displeasure and disappointment in Pastor Lenny and his wife, even though no words were spoken. It reminded me of the eerie silence right before Dad abandoned me. My shame and sense of failure overtook me when I got home, and I never returned to that church again. I couldn't bear to see Pastor Lenny's disappointed face every Sunday. Inside, I tried to be brave and justify my decision. I lied to myself about my fears and determined God had something else for me, although deep inside I felt like I had failed and disappointed God the most. I deceived myself by telling myself that this college wasn't the one I had dreamed of going to and that is why it didn't work. It was the one my pastor wanted me to attend, not me. This further justified my decision, causing me to hide from the truth. It is easy to justify our actions and hide from the truth when one is full of pain, fear, failure, and shame.

Now I was back home in the chaotic world that I hated, but knew how to survive in. Yet, without the dream that had given me hope for so long, and with a wedge between me and God for the first time, due to a deep sense of disappointment and failure, which I so desperately tried to bury. This was a new emotion in my relationship with God. My sense of His love and acceptance for me had sustained me for so long. Now, even that had changed.

≈4≈

Toxic Zone

I believed that I could never return to the church that I had attended for the past few years. My heart had been so crushed. First, being stripped of ministry because I was a girl, and then having my childhood dream end in disaster and shame. I couldn't face anyone, especially Pastor Lenny. I had determined to go forward pushing all my thoughts and feelings deep inside me like I had all my life. First things first, find a new church.

I could hear the music as I nervously walked up the steps and entered the church. It was my first time visiting this quaint church that looked like one you would see in a movie. It was a small white building trimmed in black with a bright red door sitting on a beautiful landscaped yard with a tall steeple that reached to the heavens. It was very inviting. I slowly entered the sanctuary, not sure what to expect. The music filled the room. The joy and exuberance of the congregation was like water to a thirsty soul. Pastor Gary was charismatic and very loving. I looked around and saw several young people my age; which gave me hope. By the time the service was over, I knew I had found my new home church. But little did I know the pain and darkness that awaited me.

I had only been attending the church for a few weeks when Pastor Gary and his wife, Jenny invited me over for lunch after a service. I was excited and apprehensive. I had developed such a fear of people, and yet longed to fit-in, belong, and be loved. They warmly welcomed me into their home. Jenny invited me to sit in the family room while Pastor Gary changed clothes and she finished up the last-minute preparations. I sat in the high wingback chair taking in my surroundings. Everything was clean and orderly, and it was very quiet. Suddenly, I began to experience something I had never experienced before. It swept over me like soothing cool water on a hot humid day. "What was this?" I wondered as I soaked it in. Peace! It was peace. In all my eighteen years I had never experienced peace before. I gently rubbed the arms of the chair, breathed it in deeply and sighed, "So this is what peace feels like." A warm sensation filled my soul. My life changed that day. The pain of my past, my spiritual hunger, my search for significance and this short experience of peace, caused me to open myself wide, without filters to the teachings of this church and the new path this church offered me.

My passion and love for Jesus and my need to find a new dream for my life caused me to dive into this church with both feet, hoping it would also take me far away from the pain of my past. I became involved in everything I could. I listened to every teaching I could get my hands on. This church was so different than the churches I had grown up in. The teachings were like nothing I had ever heard before. Within a year my spiritual life began to change. I was uncertain about what the changes meant. My soul was very troubled and confused, so I waited patiently after a Sunday service to talk to Pastor Gary. He was always kind, warm, and welcoming. He had one of the biggest smiles I had ever seen. He sat down next to me; he could see I was troubled. I asked him, "Why don't I pray anymore?" Growing up, prayer was my life-line, but now I found prayer to be difficult, if not impossible. Pastor Gary placed a hand on my shoulder, smiled really big, and said, "You are now getting the word in you. You are becoming mature. You don't need to pray like you used to." Mature – that was the word that hooked me. I longed to be a mature Christian woman. I was a young, wounded, vulnerable girl who took his answer to be from Jesus; not understanding that my lack of prayer was a sign that I was entering the toxic zone.

As I forged ahead into my new-found church trying to discover my way, I embraced it's teaching without hesitation. It taught about a special elect group of Christians that were better, more spiritual – the elite. According to their teaching, they were the only ones who would escape the Great Tribulation that was coming. They were the only ones who would be the Bride of Christ. Not every Christian would become a part of this group, only those who had attained that status. This teaching gave me a new dream. I was so desperate to replace the dream I had as a child, that I was willing to do whatever it took to reach that status. I wanted to be as close to God as possible. This new goal replaced the simple faith in the Jesus I had met when I was five-years old, further plunging me into the church and its teachings.

There were many new rules to learn and keep in order to reach this new status, especially for women. They even had rules on how to peel a potato. Some of these rules seemed so ridiculous that I found myself wanting to challenge or resist them, which caused my sense of failure to grow in my heart, causing me to strive even harder. I was taught that I was to be dumb and happy. That Eve's greatest sin was wanting to know truth for herself and if I wanted to know truth for myself, I was rebellious, like Eve. I began to fear reading the Bible because of the repercussions of possibly learning something for myself. Submission was a major component of their teaching. As a woman, I had very few rights. The more I strived to uphold these new teachings, the more I felt like a failure; unloved and unwanted by God. Instead of finding life, my soul and spirit were dying. I began to enter a deep depression. I found myself longing to die. I loathed myself for all my failures. All the pain from my childhood that I hoped to escape was pressing down upon me. All of this caused me to plunge even further into this radical teaching. I wanted so desperately to be loved and accepted, and I was so convinced that I would be once I attained this special status, that I didn't recognize that toxic faith was now controlling my life.

A Chance to Be Free

After a couple of years, Pastor Gary left the little church and moved to the Northwest to join another church within this small organization. The church appointed a new pastor, who within a couple of months, ran off with all the church's money, leaving the little church high and dry. Instead of sending us another pastor, the organization appointed a long-time member of the church, George, as its pastor. The enthusiasm and luster that I experienced when I first arrived at this church had faded away a long time ago. A deep sadness hung over the church. The church strived for a few more years, but never recovered from the loss of the original pastor and the theft of the second one. It dwindled down to about twenty-five faithful people, including children. So, on January 2, on my 23rd birthday, the church closed its doors. It was a sad day.

It had been five years since I walked through the doors with so much hope for my future. Now I sat bound and fettered with religious chains that had promised special status, but only produced bondage. I was alone, lost, confused, separated from everyone outside of this church, and full of fear. I knew that Jesus was still the answer, but I no longer knew how. I was filled with shame and a deeper sense of God's disappointment in me.

Here was my chance. The door to my prison cell had been flung open with the closing of the church. I was free to leave, free to go back to the simple faith I used to know. To stay within the church's organization would require me to move. I was tired of moving. I

25

wanted to stay right where I was. I wanted out and longed to be free. I tried to reengage in other churches. I went to several, but every time I entered the doors to another church I was overwhelmed with fear and panic. I had become so indoctrinated, that I truly believed I wouldn't make it to heaven if I wasn't a part of that organization. I wanted so desperately to be free from the pain and bondage, but the teachings that swirled through my head and chained my heart were too great. There was no one to help me through this process. No one who cared. I was alone and isolated. After nine months, I gave into my fears and packed up everything I owned and left all that I knew and moved to the Northwest to follow Pastor Gary and Jenny to stay in the organization. My chance of freedom was gone, there was no turning back now.

≈6≈

Toxic Move

I rushed out of the airport and hurriedly jumped into the car as the chilly wind nipped at my heels. The Northwest was so different than the plains. Jenny was there to greet me and escort me to their home. They had graciously offered me a place to stay until I could find a job and a permanent place. As soon as I got into the car, she gently took my hand, looked me straight in the eyes, and with great compassion and care said, "We know that you have experienced a lot of rejection in your life and we want you to know that we will NEVER reject you." The peace that I experienced in their living room a few years earlier flowed over me once again like a cool stream of water calming my fears and giving me a since of security, yet even this promise couldn't prevent the tidal wave of rejection that lay ahead.

Their home was nestled amongst the largest evergreen trees I had ever seen. It was a beautiful home with lots of room. I always remembered their home to be a place of peace, yet unbeknown to me, there was a storm brewing in this home that I would soon get caught up in that would change things forever.

I was excited to learn that another young girl, Leanne was also living with them. I was hopeful that we would become friends. Leanne had become like a daughter to Gary and Jenny but was rebellious against their counsel regarding a young man in the church. This kind of independent thinking and rebelliousness wasn't acceptable in their home, nor in the church. It got so volatile that Leanne moved out shortly after I arrived. This broke their hearts and sent them into such pain and sorrow that it made it difficult for them to have me living with them. My presence only reminded them of what they had lost. They began to take out their pain on me. I wasn't the young woman they wanted in their home. They wanted Leanne. I became too much of a burden for their broken hearts to bear. They asked me to leave only a few months after I arrived. I was able to get a part-time accounting job and became a live-in morning nanny to a woman in our church that had three kids.

The church in the northwest was much more connected to the headquarters of this organization. Before I was permitted to move there and be reunited with the organization, I was scored on a scale of 1-10 to determine how committed I was to the organization. I scored a 12. So, I was accepted and approved to move there. What they didn't know, was the wrestling match that had been going on inside of me for the past several months. Even though I was indoctrinated with their teachings, I longed to find freedom, hope, and life again. I longed for the simple faith in Jesus and freedom I had when I was a child. But these longings increased my sense of failure and fear of being a rebellious servant of God. I felt like a person in a dark prison cell with only a small window at the top of my cell, revealing the light outside. I was trapped. I had given myself over to their control for so long that I couldn't find my way out.

The teachings of the church in the northwest were much more intense and more advanced than they had been in our little church back home, especially in the area of submission. Submission was everything. There was a specific order to this submission. You were only responsible to submit to the person above you. It started with the Apostles, who were submitted to God. It was important to understand and believe that ALL truth came through them. There was no truth apart from what they said. Then there were the pastors, who were to submit to the Apostles no matter what. For example, if the pastor believed that something was true, he was to bring it to the Apostle, who then determined whether it was the truth. If the Apostle believed it wasn't the truth, then submission meant the pastor was to reject that notion, even if he knew it was the truth, and believe only what the Apostle said, because ALL truth came from the Apostle. He wouldn't be accountable to God for rejecting this truth because of his submission. Then in like manner, the husbands submitted to the pastor, wives submitted to their husbands, and children to their parents. Single people, like me, had to submit to the pastor and the elders in the church. The pastor was set up in such a way that he solved all the problems in the church, both within the church and domestically in people's lives. This more intense teaching on submission caused me some consternation, yet I couldn't let anyone know of the wrestling match within me, for fear of being labeled rebellious and unaccepted, and missing out on that special status that would ensure my entrance to the Bride of Christ.

Another strange and new teaching of this church was about dating. Dating wasn't allowed for fear that one would fall into sexual sin. They believed that rules would keep you righteous and prevent sin. Single people were to meet during church functions. If they felt like they met the person God wanted them to marry, they submitted it to the pastor. If he agreed, then they were to be married within six weeks.

Shortly after I moved there, I went to a church fellowship function and met this tall, handsome man, Simon. We talked the entire time. I was smitten by his looks, his personality and presence. Simon seemed to have no fear, and I was riddled with fear. I gave him my phone number but was fearful and uncertain if I had violated the rules. Simon began to call me every night and started giving me rides to work, since I didn't have a car. I found myself not caring about the rules of the church, which only gave me a greater sense of fear. Two weeks after meeting at the event, we went skiing with another couple. This wasn't considered a date, because we were with people from the church. Before moving to the northwest, I had never seen a mountain, let alone knew how to ski. It took me the whole morning to get down the bunny hill once. Simon was so patient with me, considering he had been skiing since he was five or six, and had competed in his younger years. On the ride home, he shared with me that he wanted to approach the pastor about us getting married. I agreed with him that I wanted the same. So, we decided that night to marry, confident that Pastor Bill would agree; however, Pastor Bill was leaving the next day to go to the organization's annual conference. We would keep our decision a secret and wait to ask his permission when he returned. I went home elated. I had met the man of my dreams, and yet couldn't share my good news with anyone. Joy and happiness filled my heart as I gently fell asleep. Finally, my years of pain, loneliness and rejection were over.

Simon picked me up the next day. I could tell something was wrong. We went to a nearby restaurant. He reached out to take my hand. My mind was racing. I began to rehearse all that I had learned about marriage and submission, all the rules. Two rules stuck out in my memory. First, commitment was everything, not love. Second rule was that a woman could NEVER say no to her husband, no matter what, even if it was something illegal, because she was to submit to him and him only. I had decided that since I had told him the day before that I would marry him, I was bound by these two rules – no matter what he said, I had to say yes, and I had to keep my commitment to marry him.

Simon took a deep sigh and began to tell me his secret. For the past several months he had been physically intimate on several occasions with a young girl in the church. He didn't love her or care about her. She had pursued him, and he gave into the lust of his heart. But she took it seriously. She believed that they were going to get married one day. As he shared, I discovered she was Leanne, the young girl that had lived with Gary and Jenny – the one that had broken their hearts. This was the man they used to fight over. He hadn't seen her in about five weeks. However, Leanne heard about us going skiing and showed up on his doorstep after he got home, claiming to be pregnant and threatening to kill herself. He didn't know what to do and couldn't share our decision, so he sent her to Pastor Bill because the pastor solved all the problems. As I listened to him, my heart began to break. It sank deep into the pain of my past. I wanted to run but felt I couldn't. I wanted to be angry with him, but I felt I couldn't. I was bound by the rules that I had so carefully reviewed, before he began to talk. I wanted to be a good girl, to make that special status. When all was said, I reached out with my other hand and assured Simon of my commitment to him, even though everything inside of me was screaming and crying. I performed well because I knew how to live a lie when it came to my emotions. We still longed to do things right, so we decided to not see each other again until after Pastor Bill returned and Simon could talk to him. We left there with our little secret intact. He was elated. I gave the appearance of being happy, but inside I was devastated. The joy and happiness I had felt the night before was shattered into small pieces of glass that cut into my heart, but I kept the rules.

The following week was filled with craziness. Leanne's assignment from Pastor Bill was to find out if she really was pregnant while he was gone. She was to keep it between the three of them and when he returned, they would meet and decide what to do. But that Wednesday night, Leanne came to church expecting Simon to sit with her, but he refused. She thought she had won, but she hadn't. She didn't know his commitment to me. She stormed out of the church vowing to get revenge. I got caught in the crossfires. She went to one elder after another, spilling out her pain and telling them all that she was pregnant; although, she had discovered she wasn't. On Thursday, I got a call from Gary, my former pastor who was an elder at this church. He forbade me to see Simon. He told me that if I did see him, God would kill me because that would mean I was a rebellious, stiff-necked woman. This frightened me so much. I didn't know what to do. Gary didn't know that we were secretly engaged. I couldn't say anything, but I just took the verbal abuse. I was so shaken that I called in sick and went over to talk to Shelia, another elder's wife. I also called my secret fiancé. Simon decided to come by and get me, so we could talk.

Shelia comforted me by assuring me that when Pastor Bill returned, he would fix everything.

Rumors flew through this church like a tornado through a small city. News had gotten out that we had left together. Many were convinced that we had eloped. People were looking all over for us. We had just gone for a drive to talk. We returned with the same decision we had before – that we would not see each other until Pastor Bill returned to solve everything. When we returned, we discover all the rumors and chaos that our going for a drive caused. It's like everything had blown up. I felt like I was in the crossfires of a war that I didn't want to be a part of. Someone had called Pastor Bill at the conference. They didn't feel that the situation could wait until he returned. Pastor Bill asked everyone to tell Simon to call him when we were found. Simon called Pastor Bill later that night. They talked for a very long time. He explained to Pastor Bill that Leanne wasn't pregnant. Then he explained how he wanted to marry me. Pastor Bill immediately gave his blessing, without the other issue being completely resolved. Pastor Bill assured Simon that all would be fine when he got home, and not to worry about the elders and Leanne. He would deal with them when he returned. That night we became officially engaged. I tried to pretend like my heart was elated, but I felt like I had just gotten on a train that was going somewhere I didn't want to go. I went from one prison cell to another.

Pastor Bill returned a few days later and immediately met with everyone. I was the last one he met with. He explained to me that when there is conflict like this, the most mature person was the one who had to do all the apologizing. There was that hook word again – mature. So, Pastor Bill requested that I apologize to Leanne and that I apologize to Gary. There was no discussion of how these events impacted me, hurt me, how I felt, or what I wanted. Of course, I dutifully apologized to both, wounding my heart even further.

It was during our very short time of pre-marriage counseling that I learned what kind of man I was really going to marry. Simon presented himself one way to the pastor, but I was discovering another man. He lied, cheated, deceived, manipulated and was verbally abusive. He pretended to be wealthy but was really a pauper. The more I learned who he was, the more I wanted out, but I couldn't find my way out because the neglect, chaos, abuse, and trauma from childhood had stripped me of my sense of power in decision making and there was no one to help me. Pastor Bill was determined to prove to everyone that his decision was right. Gary and Jenny were so mad at me that they no longer wanted anything to do with me, thus breaking their promise of never rejecting me, which they made when I arrived. The church became divided so much that it almost caused a church split. Leanne would come to church wearing maternity clothes and walk like she was pregnant, even though she wasn't. This drew the sympathy of others in the congregation. My shower was boycotted by some. I was caught on a battle-field with shots being fired from all directions. With every opposition, Pastor Bill became more determined to marry us. Amid this, I did the only thing I knew to do, which was to withdraw. I'd go home at night and cry myself to sleep, begging God to help me get off this runaway train, but He was silent. I didn't feel safe around anyone. I didn't know whom to trust and whom not to trust. Word had gotten out that Leanne had a plan to destroy our wedding day, so we had to have guards posted to keep her away. By this time, I just wanted to be quietly married, but Pastor Bill insisted on a big church wedding, again to prove he was right. All my childhood pain of rejection and powerlessness overtook me. My only hope was that God would do something. He would either rescue me or give me a word of comfort that He would be with me, like He was in my childhood. If He wasn't going to be, I'm not sure I would survive.

The day of the wedding came. I couldn't afford flowers, so a lady in the church went out and gathered lilacs, put them in milk bottles with pink bows on them and placed them all around the church. That act of kindness meant so much to me. It was like a cool cup of water to a very thirsty soul. It comforted me. The music began to play. I walked down the aisle with such dread, but I had one hope left. It was

33

a tradition in this church for the pastor and elders to lay hands on the couple to pray and prophesy over them during the wedding ceremony. That was my last hope. That was when I was sure God would let me know that I was going to be okay, that He would be with me as always. The time came for the prayer. We knelt, Pastor Bill and the elders laid hands on us, but there were no prophetic words, only silence. An eerie deathly silence. At that moment, I knew that God had abandoned me too. The one who had always been there for me, the one who never left my side during all the pain, chaos, and trauma from childhood, had finally left me, too. My dad had abandoned me. I was estranged from every other member of my family and Gary and Jenny, who had promised to never abandon me, had. The church had become an unsafe place and now God had abandoned as well. I was truly all alone now, without even God. All I had left was Simon. My heart died inside at that moment. After the ceremony was over, Simon looked down at me and said, "I love you." I looked at him with my phony smile and thought, "If you only you knew how I really felt."

≈7≈

A Toxic Cesspool

The wind howled through the trees blowing the fresh fallen snow off the branches, allowing it to flow through the air like it was snowing again. The sun was shining, giving the day an appearance of warmth, but the temperature was twenty-two degrees below zero; matching the coldness in my heart. I sat in our small RV trailer, forty-five miles from the nearest town. There was nothing but silence all around me, but unlike the silence I experienced so many years ago, this silence didn't bring me peace. This silence exposed the unbearable pain deep within my soul that I didn't want to feel. It was the first time that I couldn't just push it down and move forward. It was the first time that I was alone in my pain without the assurance of God's love. It had been five months since my wedding day. Out of my pain and feelings of abandonment, I had given myself over to Simon, like I had the organization. I clung to him like one clings to a root protruding from a cliff as they sway high above the abyss, hoping not to fall. I allowed him to make all the decisions for me. I followed him around like a little puppy dog. I agreed with everything he said and did. He loved being worshipped and adored like that and it made him feel powerful. His ungodly character and verbal abuse only reinforced the pain and lies that were already keeping me imprisoned. The seeds of fear that were planted in me as a child, had become full grown. I feared everyone and everything. Fear was my master and I was its slave. I had lost all sense of safety and security.

35

Shortly after we were married, I discovered that he was running from the IRS. He forbade me to take on his name and started doing business under my maiden name. We started in the business of tree planting and tree thinning. Now we were deep in the woods, in the dead of winter, to clear cut a campground. There were only sixteen people in this area and we all lived in RVs or mobile homes and traveled by snowmobiles.

The beauty surrounding me was quite the contrast to the darkness in my soul and spirit. Even though I felt that God had abandoned me, I determined I wouldn't let go of Him. He was all I had have ever held onto, I couldn't let go now. The love for Him that was planted in my heart when I was five years old was still there, but I didn't understand why my life had turned out like it did. I finally couldn't take the silence any longer and joined Simon and the sawyer with the clear-cutting job. My job was to shovel the snow from around the trees in twenty degrees below zero temperature, to prepare them to be cut down. The snow was nearly up to my waist. I was out in the woods all by myself ahead of the sawyer. The busy work kept my mind off my pain and the beauty was like a soothing balm. I saw beauty that no one else would ever see. It was the kind of beauty that only happens at that very moment, like a unique fog formation across the frozen lake, a coyote diving into the deep snow for food, or a buffalo plowing his way through the snow. I knew that God had created each scene of beauty and I drank them in like I used to drink in His presence in what seemed like ages ago. Even though I felt like God had abandoned me, I didn't realize that He was loving and sustaining me through His creation. I wouldn't have survived without His beautiful creation soothing my heart and soul.

I was far away from the organization that I had served for so many years. Its rules, in this case, worked against them. I had to leave because my husband had left. I couldn't tell him no or stand up to him. Those were the rules. I felt such fear and trepidation, but also hopeful that I'd finally be free from it. The nearest church of any kind was over a hundred miles away. The only spiritual resources I had were books and the Bible. The Bible was still hard for me to read. All I could see, when I read it were the rules, and I felt beat up rather than lifted up. So, I mostly read inspirational books.

Our job lasted a year and when it was over, I felt the tug to get back into the organization and tried to persuade my husband to move to a location where a church from that organization existed. But Simon had other plans. He remembered a church that he had attended while in college and wanted to find a place connected to it. We moved to small town in Montana and joined a small church that was part of this independent organization that he had experienced in college. I learned that this organization had a Bible school and my childhood dream peeked out, ever so small, through the darkness. Our business wasn't going well, so we decided to move to the area where the headquarters were and planned to attend their Bible school. I was slowly beginning to emerge out of the lie that God had abandoned me and felt the glimmer of fresh new hope, that maybe after all these years my childhood dream would be resurrected and come true.

We entered the church's sanctuary to discover it full of life and excitement. Behind the stage was a large open two-story room for people to pray. Many sought God before and after the services, sometimes for hours. When the services began, the pews where packed and on stage was a huge choir that sang joyous songs about God and Jesus. Many of the songs where new to me because they wrote most of their own music. There was so much life and energy in this place. I began to have hope that I would find my way back to the faith I had as a child, when I first met Jesus. We enrolled in Bible school right away; however, Simon didn't share the same passion and desire to attend as I did. Often, we'd wake up in the morning, he wouldn't want to go. He wanted to sleep in. I'd get up determined to go, but because I had given him so much power over my life, I felt chained to his choices and would return to bed with him; my heart breaking from disappointment.

Even though this church appeared to have life and good teaching, it had undercurrents of false doctrines that opened the door to a floodgate of deception that would harm many lives. Shortly after we arrived, the pastor returned from a retreat and began to introduce the congregation to a new revelation of "God's love" that they had experienced during the retreat. This love crossed all boundaries especially with the marriage relationship. This compelling love would fall on people during worship and they would enter into a worship dance with whoever "the Lord" led them to. The two would experience God's love that superseded their marriage vows. Spirituality and sexuality began to become intertwined. It was eventually taught that one could do whatever one wanted, with whomever one wanted if it was "in the Spirit." It was further taught that if the spouse was jealous or insecure, they were resisting and hindering God and that they had a demon. Marriages began to fall apart all over the church. People were leaving their spouses for this newfound, supernatural love connection.

Simon jumped in with both feet, leaving me stranded in the pews while he went off with another woman experiencing this intense love. Now the only person I had, the one I had given over my will and mind to, this root I hung onto while dangling over the abyss, was ripped out of my hands. I began to freefall deep into my pain. The further I fell, the more the church accused me of rebellion, resisting God, and having a demon. This new doctrine crashed head long into the walls of rules and doctrine from the previous organization, leaving me completely confused and bound.

It was finally recommended that I meet with one of the church's women counselors, Margret. We began to meet once a week and met for almost two years. It took me a while, but I began to feel safe with her. She was a very strong, independent woman; exactly who I needed in my life. As she listened to my story and my pain, I began to feel empowered. Because of how much I had given over my thoughts, beliefs, and decision making, first to the organization, then to my husband, I had to learn to think again, to discover myself again. I didn't know the answer to simple things like, "What's your favorite color?" She became my safe place, my place of hope and healing in the midst of my husband's verbal abuse and abandonment, because of this "move of God." He had found another woman to be with all the time "in the name of the Lord."

One night while my husband was off with that other woman, somewhere in the church (there were several areas that they allowed couples to go), a young man, Joseph, came over to me and began to love and comfort me like my heart so longed for. Margret was excited that I had finally entered "the move of God." She encouraged our relationship. I knew deep inside that this relationship was wrong, but my heart longed to be loved, and no one had loved me like Joseph. It was easy to enter this relationship and violate my conscience, when it was taught and encouraged from the pulpit. My starved unmet needs overrode what I knew to be truth in my heart.

Now Simon and I both were fully engaged in other relationships, further causing our relationship to deteriorate. We were told that if we engaged in this move of God's love, it would help our marriage and mend things. It only caused a greater wedge. Margret the counselor, and Joseph were helping me to learn to think for myself. I began to confront my husband regarding his running from the IRS and many other things. I no longer said "yes" to everything. This only escalated his verbal abuse towards me. He finally broke it off with the other woman and joined many who had left the church and began to protest what was happening. I couldn't leave and join him, because I couldn't leave the first two people who had ever really cared about me, which put a greater wedge between us.

One night, I was awakened by his car pulling up, but pretended I was still asleep. He climbed onto the bed, leaned over me and began to hit the pillow right next to my face screaming at the top of his lungs, "God, in the name of Jesus, kill Margret and Joseph. In the name of Jesus kill [so and so] in her life." He named them one by one. During that time, I had a few more friends helping me out of the abuse and pain. He kept repeating this over and over, each time he hit his fist next to my face. Fear swept through my body and I

39

knew I had to get out of the house. There had been years of abuse and control, but nothing had escalated to this extent. I grabbed the keys, ran out of the house, and hopped into my car and drove off looking to find safety.

≈8≈

But God...

The so called "move of God" swept over the church and its daughter churches like a tsunami sweeps over an island, leaving nothing behind but devastation and ruin. In a tsunami some of the people and debris get swept out to the sea, never to be seen again. Others lay dead or wounded in the aftermath, on the shore. The few that survive, with little or no wounds, are left with the mess to clean up and rebuild. This "move of God" pulverized marriages, leaving in its wake, divorces and wounded children, scared in the name of God. The storm split the church in four ways. There were those who got out of the storm and tried to rescue others. The pastor was forced to leave, taking several hundred with him to a new location, in a new town, and continued "the move." The elders were left behind to pick up the rubble, sort through the teaching, and try to restore and heal lives. Then, there were those who were swept out to the sea, no one knowing what happened to them. The church of approximately 3,500 people became a small life-boat for approximately 50-75 people hanging on for dear life.

I, like a wounded survivor of a tsunami, lay motionless on the sandy shore. Everything had been stripped from me again by the undercurrents of the storm. I was estranged from my husband. Margret had moved away to run from her pain, Joseph had left, returning to his wife and family. I was left without a church. Alone in my room, I knelt on the floor, bowed down, and let out the deepest

41

scream that turned into a gut-wrenching wail from all the pain that could no longer be contained. By now, I had been learning about the effects of trauma and abuse and realized I needed help. But where could I go? Where was it safe? I had heard of a professional Christian counselor who had helped some people who had left this church. For the first time, in many years, I made an independent decision. I decided to go see her.

I approached her office with much trepidation. I didn't know how professional Christian counseling worked, but I knew that I couldn't bear it if she told me to just trust Jesus. I still believed that He was the answer, I just didn't know how. All I had ever wanted in my life was to love and serve Him; however, the churches that I had put my trust in, had taken me down a toxic path which led to death and destruction, leaving me uncertain about truth. I entered the room slowly and fearfully. She grabbed her pen and paper, leaned forward and asked me with a cheerful voice, "How can I help you?" I looked down at the floor and wrung my hands. The words were hard to formulate, but finally I slowly said, "I need help and don't tell me, 'just trust Jesus.'" I continued to explain to her that I felt like a thousand molecules flying all over the room. No matter how hard I tried to gather them together, to form something solid, they would slip through my fingers, never forming anything of substance. Not only could I not find any stability or substance, I felt like a frustrated child who was given a toy, without instructions on how to play with it. She recognized that I was deeply wounded and provided me a safe place to talk, and talk, and talk. Week after week, I poured out my pain. Week after week, she listened. I wouldn't let her pray for me during or after the appointment, but I knew she faithfully prayed for me in between.

Shortly after I started counseling, my husband joined me. Even though Simon was a frightening man, as a Christian I felt obligated to try to reconcile with him, since he said he wanted to. He came prepared with a list, demanding that I adhere to this list immediately or he would divorce me. Some of the things on that list were egitimate, but others weren't. There were things on that list that were right, but healing needed to take place for these to be accomplished. The counselor tried to reason with him for the whole hour, but he wouldn't budge. At the end, I had to say I couldn't adhere to the list. I knew if I gave in to his demands, it would only mean going back under his control. He walked out of that appointment and straight to the courthouse the next day. My marriage was over. He left me with a huge IRS tax bill, but that was easier to live with than all the verbal abuse that I had suffered for seven years.

Over the next year all I was able to do was work and go to my counseling appointments. In between my appointments, I learned to journal, to open my heart again to hear God and read His word. At the beginning of my journey I discovered some verses in Jeremiah that described how I felt, "…Your hurt is incurable, and your wound is grievous. There is none to uphold your cause, no medicine for your wound, no healing for you. All your lovers have forgotten you; they care nothing for you…" (Jeremiah 30:12-14). I began to weep as I read these verses that described my plight. I knew that my wounds were beyond repair, beyond hope, but as I kept reading I heard the still small voice of God, "For I will restore health to you, and your wounds I will heal, declares the Lord, because they have called you an outcast: 'It is Zion, for whom no one cares!'" (Jeremiah 30:17). Even though the wounds were incurable in the natural, there was the "But God" factor that came to play.

Over the next several years, the Lord was faithful to that promise. He began to remove the toxins from my faith, giving me a new living hope. He led me through the path of healing and restoration, teaching me nuggets of truth that I often call my toolbox. The path hasn't always been easy. Sometimes I've wanted to run the other way. Sometimes things seem to be unsurmountable. Sometimes things seem like they could never change or heal. BUT God….

Part II

≈9≈

Honesty

I sat on the floor leaning against the couch, with pen and paper in hand, listening intently to the speaker. Since I was a young girl, I had known my destiny was to go to Bible school, learn God's Word, and go into ministry. That dream, along with my relationship with Jesus, was my lifeline. I was young and vulnerable when I was introduced to my church and its organization, and I was sure this church was my rescue. However, when my pastor informed me that I couldn't go to Bible school, even though the organization had one, I was heartbroken and disappointed. He explained to me that it was unbiblical to leave my church home and go away to Bible school. Being young, impressionable, and very broken, I believed and trusted him, but my hunger and thirst for learning was unquenchable. Even though I wasn't allowed to go to Bible school, my pastor made it possible for me to borrow the teaching tapes from some of the classes. I sat and listened to one tape after another. I couldn't get enough and was becoming thoroughly indoctrinated. What I didn't know, was the teaching was toxic. Instead of setting my heart and soul free, and introducing me to the Lover of my soul, the teachings were imprisoning me with legalism and faulty teaching, distorting my view of God, and creating a fear of who He was and how He would treat me.

On this particular day, I was listening to a teaching on "True Repentance." The teacher explained how if you truly repented you would never commit that sin again. If you did, then you hadn't repented. I really took this teaching to heart; however, this forced me to do one of two things: deny and hide that I had done the sin again or refrain from repenting of it until I was certain that I would never do it again. In either case, I didn't experience freedom, but rather sank into hopelessness and a deep sense of failure. This type of teaching cultivated dishonesty and fear in my life. The thought of being honest with God about my life, namely, sin, knowing that I couldn't ensure that I wouldn't do it again, caused me to develop a fear of God and how others would react to me. Jesus was no longer the answer to my sin, but someone I had to fear.

I had been taught all my life that I wasn't to lie. Lying was a sin. I believed with all my heart I wasn't a liar, so it was with great shock that I learned that I was the most dishonest person I knew. Don't get me wrong; on the outside I portrayed a very honest and noble Christian woman, but on the inside, I wasn't. Because I wanted to please the Lord so much, I learned early on, to hide who I really was on the inside. I learned the way I wasn't to be, so I denied the way I was, and presented to God and others this person I thought I was supposed to be. The legalistic and spiritually abusive teachings and communities validated this approach to God. I thought that the outward appearance was more important than the heart. I can remember people making comments about me, praising me for the virtues they saw in me, and on the inside, I would be squirming with discomfort. I wasn't that person they saw on the outside. On the inside, I was full of darkness. I became a great actress, wearing the appropriate mask, for the appropriate moment. The longer I played this role of Christianity, the more bound I became on the inside. Facing my dishonesty because of this incongruency was very hard. It required me to let go of the security of legalism, what I thought it meant to be a Christian, and face the reality of who I really was before the Lord and how He would respond to me.

My fear of how God was going to treat me and respond to me didn't start with this church's teaching. I was six years old when Grandpa came to visit us, and we were told to stay in the house. I sneaked out of the house and hopped onto the back of my girlfriend's bike. We raced down the street laughing and screaming away. Suddenly, a car turned the corner in front of us, almost hitting us. My friend slammed on her brakes and I went flying off the bike, head first, into gravel. I found my way home, barely able to see through my bloody face. They rushed me to the hospital, as I lay there on the bed and the doctor picked out gravel from my forehead, my mother leaned down and whispered in my ear, "See what God does to you when you disobey me?" In that moment, a seed of fear was planted.

I remember the first time that I was gut-level, raw honest with God about how I felt and who I was on the inside. I was driving my car down the road. I began to wrestle with this new understanding of honesty versus dishonesty. As I pondered being honest with God, I wondered what would happen to me, but I knew I had to take the risk. Mustering up all the courage I could find, I told God, "OK, I'm going to do it. Here's how I really feel." All this poison came pouring out from deep within my soul, the kind that I assumed if others knew, they would for sure be disgusted and disappointed in me. "There!" I scrunched down, wondering if lightning was going to strike. To my surprise, I felt this incredible relief. I felt like a thousand pounds had been lifted off me. I began to feel peace and hope. God now had access to that area of my heart. Now He could come in, clean out the poison, heal my heart and make me whole. Instead of discovering a stern God who was angry and looking to punish me, I discovered a loving Father, happy to come into that area and love me to wholeness.

As I read the Gospels with this new understanding, I began to see how honesty played a significant role in those whose lives were transformed by Jesus. The woman at the well-found living water when she was honest about her relationships with men. The woman with the issue of blood, received healing when she was honest about how she was the one who touched Him. The sinner on the cross entered paradise with Jesus on that day when he was honest about

47

who he was. Story after story of people's encounters with Jesus involved an honest heart, then a loving encounter with Jesus.

The pathway of untangling religious dishonesty was a long and hard one, but one worth going down. To learn to be honest in the inward part of my being took courage and a leap of faith. I had to step out of my comfort zone of religion. I had to let go of the false security of legalistic righteousness and face the truth of who I really was. I had to face my fear of being abandoned by God. I had to face pain that was hiding behind it all. Religious dishonesty filled my spirit with toxic faith and separated me from the very person I was longing to know and experience. When I was honest about my sin, I met the Savior. When I was honest about my brokenness, I met the Healer. As I became more and more honest, I began to learn how Jesus was the answer, and living hope began to arise from within.

≈10≈

Journaling

I stared at the blank page in my journal, my heart began to race, and anxiety surged through my body. I couldn't think of anything to write. I believed God had led me to this counselor, who recommended this, and I knew I had to begin somewhere, so I decided to write about the fact that I didn't have anything to write about. I had only written a couple of sentences before my anxiety grew to such intensity that my words turned into scribbling. My pen traveled all over the page making great indentations from the pressure. As I scribbled, anger began to well up inside of me until I couldn't stand it any longer. The pages flapped in the wind as I threw the journal across the room with great force and intensity. I slumped down and began to cry. "This is impossible," I thought. Hopelessness filled my soul as my tears covered my pillow that night.

My counselor understood how disconnected I was from my thoughts and emotions. My means of survival was to close everything off, compact it all deep inside of me and disassociate from it. Now, for me to receive healing and discover how Jesus was the answer, I needed to reconnect. The internal vows I had made had to be revoked. She knew that our once-a-week meetings wouldn't be enough to unlock the iron-clad safe within me. Her advice was for me to journal. I protested this exercise, explaining to her that I was an accountant. I don't do words, I do numbers. Even

49

though I was successful at writing in high school, college proved to be a different story. I flunked out of my first writing class. I allowed that failure to define me as an incompetent writer and never attempted to write again. Now my counselor was asking me to face the dread of writing. She was confident that it was necessary for my healing journey. Each day I'd sit with my journal in my lap, stare at the new blank page for the day, wanting to write, but finding that only scribbles would come out. Fear, anxiety, and sometimes anger were the only emotions I felt. I was numb to all other emotions. Eventually, my scribbles turned into words, then into sentences. Eventually, the dial on the safe turned with the right combination and the safe opened. The door was heavy, but slowly, bit by bit, the rusty hinges creaked open, and my inner being began to pour out on paper.

Day after day, week after week, I would faithfully pursue the painstaking task of journaling. The contents in the safe were old, dusty, and soiled but, little by little, everything I had placed deep within the safe came out to the light. There were days that journaling led me to places of deep pain and suffering, immobilizing and crippling me for a time. Lying on the sofa, I'd feel the pain ooze out like puss oozing out of a sore. At the same time, I'd feel the gentle love of Jesus absorbing the puss and pain into Himself. Eventually, I would recover and be able to continue my journey. Some wounds had to be treated and cared for multiple times because of how deep they were. Each time I'd journal, the path would lead me further through the wound and into the loving arms of Jesus. Sometimes journaling would take me down paths of revelation and insight that brought freedom and understanding.

Over time, journaling became my friend. It became a lifeline. It reconnected me to my story, my pain, my life, and my heavenly Father. It wasn't easy. Some days I'd cry more than I'd write. But with each journal entry more of the contents of the safe were removed until eventually, the safe itself was removed. I discovered God in the innermost parts of my being, in the ugliest places of my soul. There I ound rest, hope, and love. There I encountered the living God who bound up my wounds, renewed my soul, and breathed life into me. It was in those moments of journaling and surrendering to God that I continued to discover how Jesus was the answer. He died on the cross to take away all my pain and give me new life and hope.

≈11≈

Dialogue

I thumbed through the pages of my Bible remembering how dea
and precious it used to be to me as a child. I would read it for hours
Sometimes I'd sleep with it like one would sleep with a teddy bear
It was so alive and vibrant. I'd see new and exciting things within
its pages. I'd sense the Holy Spirit speaking to me. As a child, I
loved God's Word, but now it seemed as dead as a paper weight
For years, the Bible had been used to manipulate and control me
As I thumbed through it, I occasionally would stop and try to read
it, but the words seemed cold and taxing. There was no longer any
life in the words, just pain. With every verse I read, I remembered
the rules, the manipulation, and the messages from the pulpit about
being dumb and happy. The Bible became something I feared
instead of loved. So, here I sat, thumbing through the pages, longing
to be able to read and experience its life again. Each time I'd try to
read it, I'd only see the distorted teaching and feel the pain from the
spiritual abuse I had suffered for so many years. How was this ever
going to change? How was I going to experience life again through
God's Word?

One day, as I was thumbing through the pages, I stopped at John
8:32. It was like the words leaped off the page at me. "Then you
will know the truth, and the truth will set you free." I just kept
reading the words over and over again. The words "set you free"
echoed on the walls of my spiritual prison cell. I longed for freedom
but I wasn't free, I was bound. Freedom had been slowly stripped

from me over the years as I traded the little portions of truth I had learned as a child for the adult banquet of lies, that awaited me in toxic churches. I had entrusted truth to them, but they had betrayed me. They declared they were teaching truth and demanded that I believe their declaration of truth, but as I did, and each year went by, I became more and more bound. One toxic teaching linked to another formed a brick prison cell that seemed impossible to penetrate. That day, a glimmer of light began to shine into my cell. The sweet, still small voice of the Holy Spirit called out to me in that dark dungeon, inviting me on a journey with Him. It was a journey of discovering truth again. From that day forward, I found myself pressing through the pain, not just to read the Bible, but to dialogue with God about it. With every verse I read, I began to ask God questions and talk to Him about what it said, what I thought, and what I felt. My desire for freedom caused me to overcome my hurts and fears. "The truth will set you free" became my measuring rod to the Bible. I began to align every teaching I had ever heard to that plumb line. If I read a verse and it made me pull back, or experience the heavy weight of chains, then I knew that I was interpreting that verse incorrectly. Gently and slowly, layer by layer of false teaching, doubt, fear, and unbelief began to change to faith, confidence, and hope.

Learning to approach the Bible as a means of dialoguing with God wasn't just about peeling away false doctrines; it facilitated knowing Him and healing of deep wounds. One day, I was sitting on my couch reading my Bible. Jesus was addressing the crowd, encouraging them to ask God, to seek Him, and to pursue Him. Jesus explained how God was a very good Father. Because of who God is, we could be confident that whatever we asked we'd receive. Then I read the verses that changed my life: "Which of you, if your son asks for bread, will give him a stone? Or if he asks for a fish, will give him a snake? If you, then, though you are evil, know how to give good gifts to your children, how much more will your Father in heaven give good gifts to those who ask him!" (Matthew 7:9-11).

I just stopped in my tracks and exclaimed, "But God! My earthly father DID give me a stone and he DID give me a snake!" Tears burst forth like a flash flood through the canyon carrying debris as it flowed. As the tears subsided, I heard the Lord ask me, "What did you ask him for?" I was surprised with what came out of my mouth. It was all these intangible things. "I asked him for safety, security, acceptance." Then I heard the words, "Ask Me for those things." It had never entered my mind to ask God for them. As a matter of fact, until that moment I hadn't even realized that I had longed for my earthly father to give me those things. I slowly began to pour out my heart, asking my heavenly Father for the intangible things that my earthly father hadn't given me. Up to this point, when I had thought of asking God for things it had always been something tangible – the things you can grasp and hold, but today I entered a new realm of asking. And He responded.

God is an eternal, relational being and He created us in His image relationally. From the very beginning God desired dialogue with humanity. In the Garden of Eden, God shared unbroken fellowship with Adam and Eve, until they ate of the Tree of the Knowledge of Good and Evil. This one act damaged their relationship and their ability to dialogue with each other; and relationship requires dialogue. Throughout Scripture God is dialoguing with humanity. He dialogued with Noah about the great flood. He dialogued with Abraham on multiple occasions, but one of the greatest dialogues was regarding the destruction of Sodom and Gomorrah. He dialogued with Moses at the burning bush and on Mount Sinai. There are endless accounts of God dialoguing with humanity, but our greatest example is Jesus. He spent hours dialoguing with His father and with others. Through dialogue, Jesus learned the Father's heart and desire. One of his best-known dialogues is in the Garden of Gethsemane where He wrestled with God about His impending death. After Jesus's resurrection, He sent the Holy Spirit to dwell in us, so that we can now have unbroken dialogue with Him.

As a little girl, I naturally dialogued with God. It was instinctual. But as I became indoctrinated with toxic faith, my dialogue with God was squelched. That was the first thing I noticed, but I hadn't known to heed the warning. The more I got entrenched in toxic faith, the more I lost my ability to dialogue. Learning to dialogue with God through His Word restored the love that I had had for His Word when I was a child. I came to a point again where I cherished reading the Bible, because I knew it meant encountering God. There were some days where it was hard to press through the timbers of lies. There were some days where I did most of the talking and there were some days I just read, allowing the words to wash over me. As I learned to dialogue with God through His Word, my love for God's Word increased and the door to my prison cell opened and I began to fly with wings of living hope.

≈12≈

An Invitation

I remember a picture of Jesus that I had often seen when I was a little girl. It depicted Jesus standing at a wooden door, one hand curled up into a fist, knocking. One could sense that the knock was a gentle knock, not a forceful, demanding one. The interesting thing was that the door didn't have a handle on it. It could only be opened from the inside. The owner of the home had to respond to Jesus's knock and invite Him in, otherwise Jesus couldn't enter. This became very real to me as I began my journey out of toxic faith and abuse. I'd often come home after a counseling session reeling from the pain that had been uncovered during the session. I'd stretch out on the couch and just hurt. Similar experiences happened throughout the week for no apparent reason. I'd often come home from work and spend most of my time lying on the couch with my heart hurting. I wouldn't always know exactly why my heart was hurting, since the pain in my life was compounded. I only knew that I was hurting. At first, I would try to give it to Jesus like I had been taught to do when I was growing up, but the pain stuck to me like glue. One day, I was hurting so badly, and I was so tired of trying to give it to Jesus and failing in my attempts, that I stopped and began to do the only thing left to do - invite Him into my pain. Instead of trying to push my pain out of me and into Him, I invited Him to come into me, into my pain to heal and absorb it. This was new for me. Just like in that picture, Jesus was knocking on the painful door of my heart longing to come in, but He couldn't come in without an invitation. He had no entry unless I responded to His gentle knocking and invited Him in.

This began a new stage in my healing journey. Night after night, as I lay there in agony, I began to invite Jesus into my pain and began to experience His healing grace. It was like He was kneeling next to me and applying soothing healing ointment over my wounds. The puss drained away, the wound became a scab, and the scab became a scar. Learning to invite Jesus in transformed my thinking of His redemptive work. Toxic faith is all about what I can do, my performance, my ability to master something, my obedience to the rules. It's about me, but it's made to appear that it's all about Jesus. On this journey, I was learning that it isn't about me, but about Him and what He has done and will do. I just needed to respond to Him. It wasn't about me giving Him my pain, but about Him coming in and removing it. It wasn't about rules, it was about relationship. A relationship with Him is what was bringing about my healing and deliverance from toxic faith, which was leading me into a living hope.

≈13≈

Community

I sat on the floor praying, anxiety surging through my body. I was gaining spiritual strength and wholeness through my counseling appointments, journaling, dialoguing, praying, and readings, but I knew I was at a critical stage. It was time for me to take the next step towards my healing and discover more about how Jesus was the answer. It was time for me to reengage in the church community. It had been over a year since I stepped into the doors of a church. I rocked back and forth, memories of spiritual abuse flashing through my mind, pain surging within me screaming out "Don't go back! It's not safe! They will only hurt you!" The thought of returning to church sent shivers up my spine, yet, I knew it was time. By now, I had learned to be real and honest with God, leaning on His strength and His grace. As I cried out, I felt His gentle leading to attend a church in a nearby town. The following Sunday morning I went. I stepped into the doors, sat on the back row, and ran out the very minute the pastor said "amen." Panic and anxiety raced through my body. Out of sheer commitment to God, every Sunday I continued going to this church, kicking and screaming on the inside. Each Sunday, it got easier and easier, less kicking and screaming. My fear began to subside; I began to feel safer as each week passed.

I had been walking out my commitment to attending church for almost a year, when the gentle voice of the Spirit spoke to me and said, "I want you to change your commitment from attending the church to being in relationship with the church." Attendance was no onger enough. I needed to engage. I needed to enter into relationship with others. I needed to belong. We weren't created to live alone, isolated and alienated from Him or others. That's why family and communities can hurt us the most, but this is also why true reparative healing can only come when we are in relationship with God and others.

My first step in engaging the community of the church was to become a member. That step led me to volunteer in the Recovery Ministry at my new church. It was through belonging to this ministry that God began to use community to reveal to me more of who He was and how Jesus was the answer. The leaders of this ministry took me under their wings and loved me unconditionally. For two years, I'd go over to their home and pour out my heart, my pain, my disqualification, and more. Through their love and presence, Jesus bound up my wounds and brought forth more healing. I began to trust the church community again. I began to slowly let others in and share my life with them.

There are many "one another" scriptures in the Bible that express all the reasons we need one another. We can't truly know who we are without being in relationship with others. We can't fully experience and know the Father without being in relationship with one another. We need others for spiritual growth, for healing, for discovering our purpose, and for God to express Himself fully on this earth. God created us to be interdependent upon each other. We need each other to experience true freedom, hope and discover more of how He is the answer. I began to discover this first hand in one of our training meetings.

I entered the room with a cloud over me. I was beginning to learn to let people in but was still very cautious. When my husband divorced me, I had ended up with an IRS debt of $125,000. It was a very heavy burden and I was only able to pay $90 a month. The Lord had been teaching me many things about community, but this night He asked me to take the biggest step of faith ever. I was to tell the group about my plight and ask them to pray. The Bible says to share one another's burdens, right? As the meeting drew to a close, they asked for prayer requests. I looked down at the floor, fidgeting, and slowly raised my hand. My whole body was shaking as I vulnerably shared my story. I concluded with, "I don't have the faith for this." At that moment, a woman came over and sat next to me, put her arm around me, and said, "That's okay, I'll have faith for you." Through her faith, I felt my faith begin to receive hope. As they prayed, I began to bawl. I felt the burden being lifted by others, instead of weighing me down like a wet blanket, because I was carrying it alone. As I allowed others to help carry my burdens and have faith for me, God began to do miracles, and in nine months, I was completely free from the IRS debt.

The crippling neglect, chaos, traumas, and abuses of my childhood set me up to become entrenched with toxic faith. I was robbed of the ability to interrelate with others, leaving me vulnerable to a non-relational faith. Toxic faith isn't about relationship, but control submission and obedience to rules and regulations. It took me stepping out in faith and obedience to the Holy Spirit, and reengaging with a safe community of God, for me to discover how Jesus was the answer amidst the "one another" of the Church. This didn't happen overnight but took years of allowing the Lord to use the "one another" to rebuild my soul, my faith, my trust, and restore my hope.

≈14≈

My Receiver

With my heart racing, I slowly made my way to the front of the church auditorium. I was learning to take steps to reach out and ask for prayer support. The service had concluded, and people were milling around; some talking, some waiting, and others praying. I slowly approached the prayer pastor, every bone in my body rattling on the inside. He was a very kind and gentle man. He was easily approachable. I sat down and began to pour out my concerns, as he patiently listened. When I was done, he gently put his hand on my shoulder and began to pray. His prayers ricocheted off me as quickly as they came out of his mouth. It was obvious that my soul and spirit were an impenetrable fortress. Nothing was coming in. He paused a moment. Then began to explain to me how he felt that my receiver was broken. He compared it to a dial on the radio. There are many radio waves in the air, but the only way to hear them is to have a receiver that is set on the correct frequency. My radio receiver was broken; therefore, I couldn't receive. He prayed and asked the Lord to heal my receiver. I had lived so long without the ability to receive, that I didn't realize that I had lost it.

As I pondered what was revealed to me that night, I began to see how my childhood traumas, losses, and abuse caused me to retreat within myself and shut off my receiver. It was a survival mechanism. My environment, and the people in my life were unsafe. I had developed a belief system that everything thing was unsafe: people, animals, nature, dreams, desires, even life itself. As a child the only place I had felt safe to receive anything had been in my relationship with the Lord and at church, but as toxic faith infiltrated my life, those two places became unsafe as well. Now my receiver was completely broken.

My inability to receive showed up in many ways. I remember a time a friend of mine gave me a bouquet of flowers. The minute she left the house, I threw them in the garbage. Not out of hurt or anger but simply because I couldn't receive them. Another time, I remember going to a beautiful garden with a friend. I knew it was beautiful, not because I had an emotional response to it, but because I knew it intellectually. I remember leaning down to smell a rose. I smelled it and had no response to it. I acknowledged with my mind that it was pretty and smelled nice, but I couldn't receive the essence of beauty and how it refreshes the soul.

After the time of prayer, I went home. I sat in my living room and began to dialogue with God about this new revelation. This is the first time I had every realized that my ability to receive was broken. When you have lived without something for so long, you begin to believe it is normal. As I processed this with God and journaled about it, the Lord gave me a strategy for my journey towards healing my ability to receive. He gave me an assignment. Every day I was to sit before Him, place my hands on my chest, breathe deeply and make a conscious choice to receive. Could it be that simple? Could healing come through a simple choice of surrender. Yes. I realized I couldn' heal myself, but I could surrender to the one who could.

I began that very night with fear and trembling, because it had been a very long time since I had allowed myself to be vulnerable enough to receive. I sat in the chair, breathed deeply, and then said, "Lord, I choose to receive." I repeated it several times, taking a deep breath each time. The Lord was using the natural breathing in and receiving of air that keeps me physically alive, to teach my spirit and soul how it is done. I did this repeatedly every day for a very long time, sometimes several times a day. Also, with this new understanding I began to be intentional with my choice to receive from others as well.

no longer threw gifts away. I allowed the beauty of a flower to penetrate my senses. I allowed myself to relax when someone hugged me or touched me. At first, I felt nothing and experienced nothing. As I was faithful to this new spiritual discipline and the intentional choice to receive from others, I began to slowly receive things both spiritually and naturally. My soul began to heal, and I learned that receiving is a necessity for a healthy life; emotionally, physically, and spiritually. The chains of toxic faith that had broken down my receiver were broken, my receiver was dialed into the right frequency, and I could breathe in new faith, hope and life.

Overcoming Fear

I don't know exactly how fear became the master of my life; I only know that it began early. More seeds of fear had been planted in my young heart through neglect, trauma, chaos, and abuse than seeds of faith. These two seeds resided side by side inside of me and began to grow. As they grew, I desperately clung to the little branches of faith that were planted in my heart when I was five years old, but the weeds of fear became too many. As these weeds gained more control in the natural realm, I became a prime target for toxic faith, which slowly led me into a fear-based relationship with God, sealing the lordship of fear in my life.

The first thing that I remember being choked out of me by the weeds of fear was my ability to play. We frequently visited my cousin's farm where we would play baseball, hide and seek, explore all the barns, jump out of the rafters into the hay, and ride horses. When we weren't outside playing, we were playing games inside, or with our dolls. But as the weeds of fear grew in my heart, I found myself sitting immobilized in a rocking chair on the porch, watching others play. I'd rock back and forth, longing to join them, but unable to move. No one seemed to notice or care. In my early teens I remember a time when we went camping. My dad and sisters were playing in the water and I sat curled up on the water's edge, just deep enough that the tiny waves splashed over my shoulders. I watched with a longing heart, desiring to play but immobilized with fear. Again, it seemed as if no one noticed or cared. I felt so alone in my prison cell of fear, yet in my heart and mind I didn't feel it was safe to play, to be that carefree.

Fear continued to grip my heart as I grew. I became afraid to even try to engage with other kids in school. The pain from all the times we had moved, and the ensuing loss of friendships caused me to fear engaging because I feared the pain of loss. I became immobilized in relating to others, except with those at church. That was the only place I felt safe. But it too, became an unsafe place as toxic faith overtook my life. During the chaos and rejection that took place when I got married, the weeds of fear choked out the final sense of safety in relationships within the church. After marrying my husband and feeling abandoned by God and the church, fear was no longer just weeds in my heart. It had become a forest of trees with deep roots that clung onto my soul. I became afraid of all circumstances and all people. I couldn't trust anyone, not even my husband. I felt so alone and isolated. I was afraid to walk down a grocery store aisle if there was another person in that aisle for fear of what they would do to me. I was afraid of making a wrong decision for fear of what others or God might do to me. I was nearly completely immobilized by the time I entered my counselor's office and asked for help. I was especially afraid of God.

I was often told I had a spirit of fear that needed to be cast out. So, I would get prayer to get the spirit of fear cast out of me, but no freedom came. I would attempt to overcome fear by resisting the fear and taking authority over it but would experience very little relief. I was told that I needed to just give my fears to Jesus, but no matter how hard I tried it didn't work. I tried every Christian solution I could find, or others would tell me, but nothing set me free. They only gave me a momentary relief from fear. Then one day, while I was praying, the Lord clearly asked me, "If you could have anything in the entire world, what would it be?" I began to cry. "I don't want to be afraid anymore." At that moment, this incredible peace came over me. For the first-time, hope began to arise in my heart that I would one day truly be set free from the bondage of fear. Shortly after that time of prayer, I found myself reading a Scripture that was going to unlock the chains of fear in my life. "There is no fear in love. But perfect love drives out fear, because fear has to do with punishment. The one who fears isn't made perfect in love" (1 John 4:18). As I began to dialogue with the Lord about this Scripture, I began to realize that fear is the absence of love and the only thing that can overcome fear is love, God's love. There's no amount of casting out demons, resisting fear, or giving fear away that can permanently free a fear bound heart. Only love can set a heart free from fear. This was a new revelation and concept.

Love was more absent than present from my life through neglect, trauma, chaos, and abuse. This absence of love cultivated the soil for the seeds of fear to grow. The seeds of faith were planted during the times I had known and experienced God's love: like when I was five and sitting on my dad's lap, when I was baptized in the chilly waters of Center Creek, and the many times I ran into the arms of Jesus as a child in the privacy of my room. Worship, prayer, and reading God's Word had cultivated the soil in my heart for the seeds of faith. When I became indoctrinated with toxic faith, the branches of God's love were clipped off. I could no longer pray or read my Bible, and worship was very weak. The small portion of God's love that I had experienced was choked out and I lived a life full of fear of being punished.

God had prepared me for this moment. He had put into place tools that I would need in order to be able to receive His love and be free from fear. I had to get past the emotion of fear, stop hiding behind it, and face it with an honest heart. I would journal and face the reality of the absence of love in my life. I dialogued with God through His word on the subject of "Do not be afraid." When I recognized fear in my life, I acknowledged this was an area in my life where love was absent. I would invite Jesus to pour out His love into the area of fear and I would practice receiving by laying my hands on my heart breathing in deep breaths of air, which emulated the receiving of God's love into that area of my heart. It was the beginning of a ourney of my heart receiving God's perfect love and the chains of fear being broken.

Seeds of faith began to be planted in my heart again through the love I experienced in counseling, worship, reading God's word with dialogue, praying, and community. These seeds of faith began to grow and choke out the weeds of fear, so much so that in just a short-time after this revelation, I was able to travel to a foreign country by myself, without fear, to visit a friend. While there, my heart felt like it would burst with overwhelming joy and gratitude. I never dreamed I could be this unafraid and yet, I knew that this was just the beginning of the journey and living hope rose up in my heart.

≈16≈

Heart Set Free

I entered the room slowly. My heart was filled with both anticipation and apprehension. The prayer team greeted me with warm embraces and invited me to sit in what they lovingly called "the hot seat." Receiving prayer from this group had become an important part of my healing process through community. Today my heart was full of pain and anxiety over my earthly father's abandonment. As they prayed and waited on the Lord, I could feel God's peaceful presence. They tenderly and patiently allowed me to fully express my pain and hurt. When I was all finished, the leader leaned over to me and said, "Cathy, Jesus didn't just die for the sins you committed, but He died for the sins committed against you so that your heart could be set free." I looked up puzzled by what he said. Until this very moment, I had only understood sin as something I committed and for which I desperately needed forgiveness. As the leader began to expand on what he meant, it gave me a greater understanding of sin and the power of the cross and the resurrection. When my earthly father abandoned me, he sinned against me. According to Romans 6:23 "the wages of sin is death…" and sin always demands a payment. When my earthly father sinned against me, this sin produced death in my soul, causing ruin and destruction in my heart. I learned that Jesus died for this sin (my earthly father's abandonment) on the cross so that I could receive life in this area where sin had produced death and destruction. This understanding of sin and the power of the cross over it allowed me to receive what Jesus did in a

68

greater dimension. I no longer saw the events in my life merely as neglect, trauma, chaos, and abuse, but began to understand them as sins committed against me, and for which Jesus died so that my heart could be set free.

When I began to understand that my earthly father sinned against me, I realized that his actions towards me were also against God. This meant that he was going to have to stand before God and answer for what he had done. Realizing this empowered me to let go of hurt, pain, and unforgiveness. I was no longer alone in my pain; God had risen up and addressed it on the cross. He became my advocate. I remember visualizing my earthly father standing before God as I processed the pain from the sins, he committed against me. I no longer had to be the judge. I had a righteous and fair judge who cares about both my earthly father and me equally. He extended forgiveness to my earthly father and healing to me. If my earthly father would've been alive, God would've also extended restoration to us.

I learned that if I called the actions against me as something other than sin, my heart would continue to stay bound. I learned that if sin isn't the problem, Jesus isn't the answer. Going beyond psychological terms and identifying actions against me as sin was challenging at first, because of my misunderstanding of the word "sin" and how the word had been used to control me in toxic faith. But when I began to learn that sin wasn't about breaking rules, but rather about whatever harms relationship, I embraced using this term to identify what had happened to me and discover how Jesus is the answer.

It didn't just end there. The leader, during another prayer session, also showed me that I needed to know God the Creator, not just the Creator of the universe, but the God who creates in me that which wasn't there. He wanted to give me new life by creating in me that which would've been there if the sins committed against me had never happened.

God's design is for our parents to impart certain things within us that enable us to grow into healthy, whole adults. When they sin against us, destruction happens, the things we need aren't imparted and sometimes even what gets imparted, is robbed from us. Jesus died on the cross, breaking the power of that sin over our life. Now God wants to come in and give us life by creating that which would've been there if the sin had never happened. He doesn't want us to just learn to cope with what happened. He wants to heal us and set us free as if it never happened. That is how complete God's work of grace is.

Now I understood why I had felt like a thousand molecules flying all over the room, without any form, when I had first met my counselor. During those prayer times, hope rose in my heart to a new level. I didn't just apply this truth to my earthly father's actions, but to all those in my life who had sinned against me in many ways, big and small. Each time I experienced the crippling effects of the sins sinned against me, I would pray and ask God to show me how to appropriate the work of the cross in that area of my life. I'd stand on the promise that Jesus died for that specific sin to set my heart free. Sometimes it would feel like I was "white-knuckling" it as I stood in faith. I then began to ask God to create in my heart whatever would've been there if the sin hadn't been committed against me. As I was able, I would get as specific as possible about the sin, the impact, and what had been lost or destroyed. Sometimes I could identify the sin, but didn't understand really what I had lost, but God did. As I learned to pray and interact with God at this level, miracles began to happen in my life. The thousand molecules flying all over the room began to come together and take shape. I began to experience a solidness and wholeness that only comes from God's creative power and love. The power of death that had been released in my heart the moment someone sinned against me had now been replaced with the power of the cross and the resurrection. These were times of supernatural acts that transformed my shattered, wounded heart to a heart full of life bringing me out of the bondage of toxic faith into a place of hope.

≈17≈

Expect Restoration

The children were playing in the gym waiting for their parents to pick them up. I sat across the foyer, taking it all in and enjoying watching them laugh, play, and run around. They were so joyful and innocent. A little girl saw her father walk into the gym. Her eyes got big. Her face became radiant with a huge smile. She ran full-speed into his arms. He lifted her high above his head, brought her down for a nose rub, and then embraced her with a firm but tender, loving embrace. Even though I had experienced a lot of healing by now, I couldn't help but wonder what it would've been like to have experienced a loving father like that in my childhood. At that moment, I heard a gentle whisper, "I will repay you for the years the locust has eaten…". I knew immediately that this was from a very familiar verse, Joel 2:25. At first, I shook it off because it was such a familiar verse to me, but then this confident assurance arose inside of me. I knew that this was a promise from God to me. He wasn't just interested in healing me, but He was also intent on restoring what I had lost.

I went home, sat down at my computer and began to make a list of all the things the locust had eaten – all the things I had lost due to neglect, trauma, chaos, abuse, and years in toxic churches. Then I made a second column and declared what it would look like to have them restored. I printed out the list and hid it away. Since then, I've experienced restoration beyond what I could have asked, thought, or imagined.

Among the many things I wrote that night, three stand out that want to share with you:

The Years Stolen	The Promised Restoration
Marriage: the years of marriage to the same man that God gave me, the years of my heart's desire being met, the years of not being alone, the years of being loved and cherished, and the years of being cared for.	I desire the second marriage that God promised me. A good & healthy marriage where we meet each other's needs and communicate well. We would be best friends.
Children: the years of bearing a child – having one formed in my womb, knowing the blessing of having a quiver full, years of being a mom, and years of experiences with a husband, who was a good father.	I would like to marry a man who has children who would accept and love me and let me have a role in their lives. Not to replace their mother, but to add to them. I want to marry a man who is a good father.
Education: the years of Bible school and theological education. Learning and growing in my understanding of God.	I want to go back to school and get my master's degree in Pastoral Care. I want to be maximized by God.

Several years into my healing journey, I began to feel that it was time for me to remarry. This was a very scary thought and I knew that I was going to need help from my counselor and the community around me to be able to move forward. God sent me a wonderful woman who felt called by God to meet with me every week to pray with me for a husband. We met for almost a year and watched God unfold the story.

I was encouraged to make a list of what I desired. Again, this was difficult because it involved such a vulnerable part of my heart. I wasn't sure what to ask for because of my history, so I asked God to give me the more – to give me what I couldn't imagine or think because with my history what I could imagine, or think was so much less than what God could do (Ephesians 3:20). I also used the list of qualities that are given in the Bible for leaders (1 Timothy 3:1-10). Since this is what God values, it is what I would value, too. One of those items on the list is a man of good reputation.

I met Stephen during a meet and greet time at church, but it took me three years to open my heart to the possibility of dating him. At the right time, God miraculously showed both of us that He was bringing us together. After we began dating, one person after another come up to me and told me how much they loved him, then they proceeded to tell me these incredible stories of behind-the-scenes things he had done. God revealed to me that Stephen truly was a man of good reputation. We were married later that year with a great celebration. In choosing this man for me, God restored what I had lost. Stephen loves me and cherishes me beyond what I could've ever imagined or thought. We are best friends and love life together. He is also a good father.

Stephen brought two beautiful girls into our marriage, Chandra and Syona. They both have allowed me into their hearts and lives in many ways and degrees. I never knew how much I'd enjoy loving two wonderful girls and being there for them. The greatest miracle of this restoration is something I had buried deep in my heart. As a young girl growing up, I had a desire to adopt a little girl from India. I had desired it more than having my own child, but I had forgotten about it until one day I watched Chandra jump out of the car with her friend and go excitedly into the school all dressed up for the dance. They pranced into the building all excited, giggly and talking. As I watched them, the memories of my heart's desire flooded my soul, I heard the Lord say to me, "This is your little girl from India". She had been adopted from India by Stephen and his first wife. I began to cry and experience overwhelming joy and gratitude. God is so good. His restoration was beyond what I could have imagined or thought. He didn't just give me two wonderful daughters, He gave me a desire of my heart that had been buried. Both have grown up to be beautiful, wonderful ladies who have married and started their own journey with their husbands. I also have two grandchildren, Clover and Kyrie that I love deeply and another on the way that I can't wait to hold and love. I am thankful for the girls allowing me to be a part of their lives.

I struggled for years from the pain and agony of not going to Bible school right out of high school. I had lost all hope of ever getting a Bible education and had finally made peace with that reality. Then one day, our senior pastor announced to the staff pastors that he would no longer sign-off on our license renewal if we didn't get an education. He wouldn't dictate to us what level of education we had to have, just that we had to get some education. At first, I began to attend a Bible institute, but found it to be unfulfilling. The director over me encouraged me to inquire about getting a master's degree. At first, I resisted because I couldn't see any way it could happen since I didn't have a bachelor's degree. I learned; however, that I could apply to be admitted as a special status student. I did and was accepted. I began to work on my Master in Pastoral Care, but within a year felt redirected to get a Master of Divinity. As I completed my master's degree, I was offered a scholarship for the doctorate program. Again, God's restoration was beyond what I could have imagined or thought. My idea of restoration was a Master in Pastoral Care. God's idea was a Doctor of Ministry.

I wrote down many things that night, so many years ago. Many of the items I wrote down have been restored to me in ways that I couldn't have imagined or thought. There are still other items that I am waiting for the restoration, but know that they, too, will be restored beyond my expectation. This relational journey with God that began by learning to be honest, has taken me far from the toxic faith of expectations, performance, control, fear, and strict adherence to rules, to experiential restoration, far exceeding everything that had been stolen from me. My heart is full of a living hope for today and tomorrow.

Embrace the Journey

I nervously opened the door to the Fireside Room hoping to find some familiar faces, if not, at least some welcoming ones. I decided to take another big step to engage in community by attending a single's meeting, unaware that it would change my life. Everyone was milling around chatting, happy to see one another. I shyly sneaked around the various groups and found a seat. The leader gathered everyone in a big circle. After we sang a few songs, the leader asked us to close our eyes and imagine what it would be like when we saw Jesus for the first time. I closed my eyes and saw Jesus standing there with big, open arms. His face was beaming with joy and excitement. Just like the little girl in the gym, my heart filled with joy when I saw Him, my face became radiant with a big smile, and I ran full-speed into His arms. He tightly embraced me and began to weep. His tears were tears of boundless joy and great relief. As He held me close and wept, I heard Him say, "Now, now, I get to completely deliver you." Then He sighed and began to weep some more. At that moment, I understood that it wasn't until we leave this world and enter His embrace that we will be completely free. While here on earth, we are on a journey towards this momentous day of deliverance and freedom. As we follow Him, we will experience healing, forgiveness, wholeness, restoration, and grace to greater depths with each passing day, but our final and glorious deliverance and healing will be when we see Him face-to-face.

Several years ago, my husband and I went with some friends of ours to Great Britain. We met for a year to plan our trip. We painstakingly researched out each destination and all the places we wanted to see. The final plans were made, and each destination was determined. When we got our rental car, we were surprised to discover that it had a GPS navigator in it. We lovingly called her, Navie. Our first planned destination was Bath. On the motorway, it is a straight shot from London to Bath. But instead of going that route, we decided to pick a city on the map in the middle of nowhere, have Navie direct us to that city, and then once there, instruct Navie to direct us to Bath. We used this method throughout our trip to travel to the various destinations we had predetermined. As we trusted in Navie and let go of our focus on specific destinations, we experienced and explored England and Scotland in ways that we couldn't have dreamed or imagined when we planned the trip. Our trip, that started as a trip of specific destinations, became a journey of unparalleled adventure, beauty, challenges, and deepening relationships. We went from the southernmost tip of England to a northern point in the highlands of Scotland. There were unexpected joys and adventures as we followed church bells from the motorway to discover a quaint small town, took an unknown tiny road up a steep hillside to discover an old church and cemetery, of which we learned later that it had been used in a famous television series. We visited the beautiful, picturesque small town of Killin, Scotland, which we didn't even know existed when we so strategically had mapped out our trip. We went through winding, one lane roads, highways that looked like alleys, rolling countryside with rock walls, and drove through steep gulches. We saw beauty that we wouldn't have seen on the motorway. This one, unexpected piece of electronics changed the whole course of our trip. Instead of a trip focused on going from one destination to the next, Navie became a tool that turned the trip into a journey of unparalleled experiences. We no longer worried about where we were going, because Navie knew the way.

As I stepped into my counselor's office for the first time, remember telling the Lord that I was going to do this, take care of it and move on. I saw it as a destination, not a journey. Destinations are places you plan to go to, places you arrive at, and places you leave behind. A destination is something you attain. A destination can be a place where you plant yourself, never to move from again. Destination is something you control. A journey, on the other hand, is movement. It ebbs and flows around the terrain of life, like a river. Each new bend presents a new course, sometimes the river flows smoothly and other times there are rapids, but it is continuously flowing. If it doesn't continue to flow, it becomes stale and brackish, losing its life-giving properties. My life in the toxic faith churches had been all about destinations rather than a journey. I had been constantly attempting to arrive through performance. I feared wouldn't make it to the right destination. I didn't see God as someone to journey through life with, but someone to fear and appease. The river that had flowed through me when I was five had stopped flowing and had lost its life-giving properties.

Even though I started out approaching it as a destination, my journey began that night, when I took a leap of faith and stepped into my counselor's office even though everything inside of me wanted to run. Through her years of wisdom, counsel, and care, along with those in my community, I learned the steps of honesty, journaling, dialoguing, receiving, and much more. The chains of toxic faith weren't broken by another form of religion, but rather a dynamic relationship with the living Christ. It was a relationship that had begun when I was five years old but had been thwarted by the sins of those who sinned against me in many ways. But God... He saw my incurable wounds and declared He would heal them. He didn't just heal them, He restored me to places I never dreamed or thought. went from toxic faith that was brackish and stale to a journey flowing with living water.

On our trip, Navi was our guiding light that kept us on track as we adventured daily into the unknown. I can still hear its British accent saying, "At the roundabout take the third left." Without Navi our trip would've been limited and nowhere near as eventful or fulfilling as it turned out. In our relationship with God, we are given a Navi, the Holy Spirit. He is there to tell us which way to go, how to maneuver through the highway that really looks like an alley. He will answer our questions, and comfort us when we hit "road ruts." He promises to always be there; we just need to seek Him and invite Him in. He is our constant companion as we embrace this journey with God to wholeness, life, and a living hope. While on earth we are on a journey, but we will arrive at our destination when we see Jesus face-to-face, when He holds us tightly in His arms, filled with joy and relief, and says, "Now, now I get to completely deliver you." What joy we will experience on that day. Until then, we embrace the journey with God, today and every day. If you haven't already begun your journey, I invite you to begin your journey with Him today, invite Him into your life and listen to His still small voice. You will go on an unparalleled journey with Him and He will give you living Hope.

36902950R00049

Made in the USA
Middletown, DE
20 February 2019